WILDLIFE
FACT·FILE
yearbook

·1993·

Foreword by
Craig
Tufts
*National Wildlife
Federation*

Includes an interview with
Gerald
Durrell

First published in the U.K. in 1992 by International Masters Publishers Ltd.
Winchester House, 259–269 Old Marylebone Road, London, NW1 5RW

U. S. Edition Copyright © 1993 International Masters Publishers Ltd.

"Monitoring Manatees," page 180: Copyright © 1992 by The New York Times Company.
Reprinted by permission.

Edited, designed, and produced by International Masters Publishers Ltd., London.

Publishing manager	*Deborah Clarke*
Editor	*John Birdsall*
Editorial consultant	*Jonathan Elphick*
Deputy editor	*Matthew Turner*
Subeditor	*Amanda Coe*
Art editors	*Colin Hawes, Frank Landamore*
Designer	*Keith Davis*
Illustrator	*Steve Kingston*
Picture editor	*Mira Connolly*
Picture researchers	*Jackum Brown, Vickie Walters*
Senior production controller	*Suzie Hutton*
Production controller	*Stefan Podhorodecki*

U.S. Edition:

Editorial Director	*Jane Ross*
Produced by Roundtable Press, Inc., New York	
Directors	*Marsha Melnick, Susan E. Meyer*
Project Editors	*Sue Heinemann, Alice Quine*
Assistant Editors	*Karen Hammonds, Amy Handy*
Designer	*Martin Lubin, Binns & Lubin*

Printed and bound in the United States by Arcata Graphics Company.

Consultants
John Farrand, Jr.
Author and adviser for the National Audubon Society
Dr. Pat Morris, B.Sc., Ph.D.
Lecturer, Department of Biology, Royal Holloway and Bedford New College
Bob Scott
Head of Reserves Management, Royal Society for the Protection of Birds
Dr. M. A. Taylor
Assistant Keeper of Earth Sciences, Leicestershire Museums Service

The publishers would like to thank Hal Robinson, Sydney Francis, Dr. Tony Hare,
John Farrand, Jr., Judy Karpinski, Craig Tufts, and Lynn Bowersox
for all their help and advice in producing this book.

ISBN: 0 9518566 2 6

WILDLIFE FACT·FILE
yearbook

1993·

Overleaf: *The tusks of a walrus have many good uses. They help it clamber over ice, and they serve as dueling weapons when males fight for a mate.*

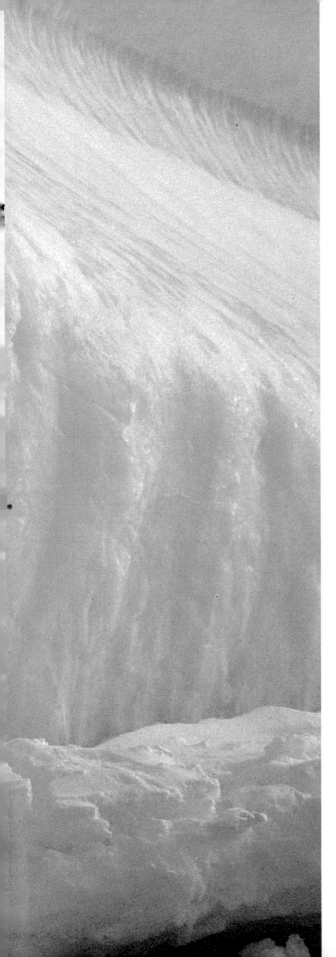

CONTENTS

FOREWORD

Looking through this book, I have a good feeling. People *are* making a difference, even though we still face major problems in dealing with habitat loss and restoring endangered species. At the 1992 Rio Summit the world took notice that we *must* put our house in order for our own survival and to protect the millions of other species that are critical players in planetary life.

I treasure books like the *Wildlife Fact-File Yearbook*. The current volume provides incredible images and adds to my understanding of environmental issues. Facts like the ones in this book are building blocks that sustain our interest and spur our actions. They are the gnats and leafy matter at the base of the thought chain.

As you page through this book, the natural world comes alive. I hope that this is an inducement to experience wildlife firsthand. Nature's biggest surprises and most important lessons come when we are physically immersed in its scents, sounds, tactile sensations, and stunning visual imagery. For children and adults alike, a backyard wildlife habitat or an undeveloped lot along a stream presents an unequaled learning opportunity. Even more important, it allows us to be personally involved with our non-human neighbors on earth.

Our future depends on taking responsible actions in our everyday lives. Supported by facts and experiences and fueled with emotion, each of us can make a difference. Enjoy this book—then go out and plant a meal for a butterfly, give songbirds clean drinking water, or replace a tidy lawn with native plants. Begin by taking a stand for wildlife at home and move on from there.

Craig Tufts

Craig Tufts, *National Wildlife Federation*

Above: *Craig Tufts has been working on conservation issues for the National Wildlife Federation since 1976. He currently directs NWF's Backyard Wildlife Habitat Program.*

Left: *The dew of a summer morning frosts the fine hairs of a buff-tip moth caterpillar. The adult that finally leaves the pupa is patterned to look just like a chip of birch wood.*

7

INTRODUCTION

Each year brings a new *Wildlife Fact-File Yearbook*. This year's volume offers an abundance of fascinating insights into the natural world. You can learn, for example, about important recent efforts to reduce the threats that bears and wolves face. Or you can find out about scientists' thrilling new discoveries about pterosaurs, the extraordinary winged reptiles that last flew some 65 million years ago.

Through its clear, lively text and beautiful illustrations, this book provides an up-to-the-minute picture of wildlife in all parts of the world. One photo essay explores the intriguing question of how animals move, while another focuses on gorgeous birds of paradise and their bizarre courtship displays. Yet another article reveals the secrets of life high in the rainforest canopy.

In this volume you have the chance to visit the realm of the gray whale—the most primitive of all living whales. You are also invited to step into the "sixth dimension" and learn about new discoveries concerning the extraordinary senses that many living creatures possess. In addition, you can explore the world of falconry and the way this sport is helping conserve some of the most threatened birds of prey.

There are hard-hitting analyses of the accomplishments of the 1992 Earth Summit in Rio de Janeiro, the effects of tourism on the environment, the impact of conservation programs on indigenous people, and the problems created by the expansion of modern fisheries. A report on forests in the West underlines how their deteriorating health, combined with a six-year drought, has greatly increased the risk of fire. In a different vein, a look at the wonders of the Galápagos Islands highlights the problems this real-life paradise is facing. If you would like to observe nature closer to home, there are instructions on how to encourage wildlife in your own backyard.

Several essays explore different conservation organizations' efforts to protect the environment. Profiles of the National Wildlife Federation and the National Audubon Society describe how they are preserving diverse animals, plants, and habitats all over the United States. A portrait of the Mississippi River Revival shows how grass-roots efforts can help save a river, and an account of Greenpeace reveals activists' success in focusing media attention on environmental abuses all over the world.

A story on Belize's efforts to save the jaguar and its jungle habitat stands as an example of how the policies of even one country can make a difference. There is also a clear discussion of international wildlife law and the difficulties of enforcing some of the existing treaties.

An informative article introduces some of the 19th-century pioneers of natural history. The excitement of recent research is conveyed in a report on an ongoing investigation of Florida manatees. In a candid interview Gerald Durrell, the well-known writer on animals, offers a close look at the work of his zoo, the Jersey Wildlife Preservation Trust. A wildlife warden in Africa and a wildlife sound recordist also talk about their experiences.

The Green Pages at the end of the book feature a calendar of events affecting wildlife and the environment over the past year. Other elements in this fact-packed section include listings of conservation organizations and new books and videos.

For everyone who is interested in nature, the *Wildlife Fact-File Yearbook* is an indispensable guide to understanding the latest developments in the amazing world of wildlife. Enjoy it.

Far left: *The rainforests of Belize in Central America are host to the tiny red-eyed tree frog.*

ANIMALS OF THE WORLD

Life on earth began over three billion years ago. Between then and now, millions of species have evolved—some only to become extinct and some that have yet to be discovered by humans. Among the most adaptable species are bears, and this section opens with a look at the latest research on both black bears and grizzlies.

We also examine the remarkable senses that give many animals the edge necessary for survival; look at the spectacular birds of paradise, which have fascinated people for centuries; and then focus on the tenacious gray whale, which has twice recovered from the brink of extinction. Next, we explain the perilous migrations of birds and then the mysterious ways in which animals move.

We offer a glimpse into the centuries-old traditions of falconry, and then we bring a more distant past to life with a report on research on the pterosaurs—winged reptiles that ruled the skies long before modern birds. We approach the end of this section with a look at present-day efforts to restore the endangered gray wolf and then conclude with a novel view of life in the world's rainforests, as seen from high above the ground.

Above left: *The mountain gorilla's aggressive demeanor conceals a shy nature. This endangered mammal continues to suffer from the clearance of its habitat by humans.*

Above: *Once common in much of Europe, the red kite has suffered severely as a result of overhunting. Despite conservation efforts, the bird remains rare.*

Left: *The loggerhead turtle's huge flippers propel it through the warm waters off the coast of Florida.*

BEAR ESSENTIALS

Above: *The Kodiak bear of Alaska is the largest grizzly bear subspecies.*

Right: *Bears are the largest living land carnivores. However, size does not guarantee survival, as researchers are discovering.*

Time is running out for the world's bears. The effects of habitat destruction and poaching threaten to eliminate most bear populations during the next 20 to 30 years. This bleak possibility created a solemn mood at the Ninth International Conference on Bear Research and Management held in Missoula, Montana, in February 1992. Over 400 biologists gathered to exchange ideas and the results of their latest research. But amid the excitement of sharing new insights, concern grew as it became clear that conditions for bears, especially black and grizzly bears, are rapidly deteriorating.

To make conservation effective, a solid foundation of good research is essential, but black and grizzly bears are among the more difficult mammals to study. They are often found in remote locations living far apart, tend to be secretive by nature, and are dormant during the winter when visibility is best and good tracking snow is present. What's more, when they are visible they are potentially dangerous. It isn't surprising, therefore, that the study of bears has lagged behind other areas of wildlife research.

Through the 1950s knowledge of bears was limited to the observations of naturalists and hunters and what could be deduced from droppings, signs, and the carcasses of dead animals. In the 1960s, however, scientists began to develop the radiotelemetry equipment and tranquilizing drugs that have since revolutionized practical research. Over the last two decades the number of biologists armed with these new techniques and working on bears has greatly increased, resulting in a proliferation of research and publications. Unfortunately, the threats to bears and their habitats have grown far faster than our knowledge of how to diminish them.

Worldwide, six of the eight bear species are faring poorly—only the American black bear and the polar bear are relatively secure. The grizzly, known in Europe and Asia as the brown bear, is the most widely distributed species and, though doing well in certain places, is facing serious threats in other areas. Almost all bear research to date has been done on the black and grizzly bears of North America, and North American experts have helped start telemetry studies on brown bears in Spain, Sweden, Croatia, and Mongolia.

Techniques to capture and tag bears are now routine, thanks to the pioneering efforts of many biologists. Early drugs were dangerous, both to bears and biologists. Doses were unreliable, and bears would suddenly awaken during the collaring procedure—an alarming experience for bear and biologist alike! Drugs are now used with a wide safety margin; they can tranquilize a bear in three to eight minutes and allow it to recover slowly after an hour.

Below: *A researcher weighs a young cub taken from its winter den. The cub is returned to its mother unharmed, and the data is recorded for future reference.*

In open terrain bears can be darted with a tranquilizing gun fired from a helicopter. Where thick cover and trees interfere, a bear can be trapped in a large barrel or a

culvert-style trap, with a door triggered by the bear tugging at sacks of bait hung in the rear of the trap. The bear is safely held until it can be injected with a syringe on a pole.

Researchers examine, weigh, mark, and radio-collar the immobilized bears before releasing them. The collared bears can be located and followed from the air using special radio receivers. Collar batteries last for over two years, and by changing collars before the batteries wear out, it is possible to track individual bears for many years. This monitoring provides information on movements, habitat use, breeding, rate of reproduction, and survival.

Permanent marks such as ear tags or tattoos can also generate useful information.

Above: *Teeth provide important information about a bear's age. Data can be taken from a live, immobilized bear—as shown here—or from the carcass of a dead animal.*

Left: *In areas that sustain remnant bear populations, the actual bear density—measured as the number of bears per 200 square miles, for example—may be very low.*

A female Kodiak bear killed last year by a hunter had been tagged as a youngster in 1958. This 35-year-old bear is the oldest wild bear yet documented. Unmarked bears can be aged by their teeth. A small premolar tooth—when extracted, sliced, and stained—reveals a series of lines like tree rings. These are called *cementum annuli* and correspond to the bear's age. Cementum studies suggest that bears in the wild normally live only into their 20s and that females tend to outlive males.

In the early 1900s, biologists described dozens of species of grizzly bear in Alaska alone, sometimes basing each definition on the discovery of a single skull. It is now generally accepted, however, that only one species of brown, or grizzly, bear, *Ursus arctos*, exists in North America, Europe, and Asia. Studies of undisturbed populations of grizzly bears in Alaska are using new DNA techniques to determine the extent of genetic variation within and between areas. This is important when trying to save small populations such as those in Europe. For there is a fear that among remnant populations of bears, inbreeding could make future generations less viable. These concerns have prompted biologists to consider introducing unrelated individuals into small populations to maintain genetic diversity.

Much research on both black and grizzly bears concentrates on habitat relationships, for the habitat contains all that is necessary

persists in the face of some habitat alteration, there seems to be a threshold beyond which recovery is impossible. It is difficult to know what the threshold is or even when it has been passed because individual bears may continue to inhabit an area even after a viable population is lost. Human settlements often carve bear habitat up into smaller and smaller chunks until it can no longer support a bear population.

Uncontrolled killing by humans is also contributing to the demise of bears. These animals mature slowly, with females producing their first litters at six to eight years old. They then keep their offspring with them for two to four years. Even if they live to be 20 years old, they may produce only a few litters in their lifetime, and cub mortality in the first year is high—typically 25 to 50 percent. One Alaskan study that followed 11 female grizzlies from sexual maturity to their death found that each bear produced an average of two surviving yearlings during its life. The projection of data from these kinds of studies into computer models has demonstrated how sensitive bear populations can be to mortality. With-

Above: *The grizzly bear's name refers to the silvery tips on the hairs of its coat.*

Right: *Bears are quite intelligent—smart enough to develop hunting techniques. Individuals learn from experience which places in a river are best for catching fish.*

for the survival of bears in an area. Recent studies documenting the food habits and habitats of bears reveal an amazing adaptability. Because of climate and vegetation, grizzly bears in southeast Alaska depend on stands of old-growth temperate rainforest, whereas other grizzlies in northern Alaska thrive hundreds of miles north of the tree line. Black bears throughout North America are closely tied to forested areas, yet new work done in Labrador has found black bears living on the treeless tundra, having moved into areas where grizzly bears had been exterminated.

The adaptability of black and grizzly bears is cause for hope, but human activities do take their toll, and the impact tends to be cumulative. Even if a bear population

out overhunting by humans there is not a problem, since bears evolved with few other enemies and natural mortality rates for mature animals are fairly low.

In another area of research, unraveling the mystery of bear hibernation remains a challenge. When biologists peer into black bear dens before immobilizing the animals, they are privileged to witness one of the most remarkable physiological feats in the mammal world. In these small, grass-lined chambers bears may spend six to eight months without eating, drinking, urinating, or defecating, yet without significant loss of bone or muscle. Strictly speaking, a bear doesn't hibernate since its body temperature hardly drops and it can wake when disturbed as if it had only been asleep. Remarkably, bears in a dormant state detoxify and recycle metabolic waste and continue to build bone. How females combine hibernation and pregnancy is another mystery waiting to be investigated.

Recent work suggests that serum from hibernating bears injected into white rats and even monkeys can elicit a slight metabolic response. More work is needed, but

the possibility that other nonhibernators may possess receptors for the hibernation trigger is exciting. Other work on the medicinal properties of bear gall has resulted in the synthesis of a drug used to dissolve cholesterol gallstones. Physiologists are also trying to isolate the substances that allow bears to hibernate so successfully. Doctors are hopeful that breakthroughs in the treatment of kidney disease and osteoporosis may result from research now being conducted. Some scientists even feel that it will eventually be possible to induce a state akin to hibernation in humans taking part in extended space flights.

Every study of bear behavior has demonstrated the extraordinary individuality, intelligence, and adaptability of bears. Members

Above: *It is second nature for the curious cubs to explore their environment. This is not a problem in a purely wild habitat; however, dangerous encounters can occur in places where humans visit or settle.*

17

Right: *Play is only one part of the learning behavior of these complex mammals.*

of family groups exhibit distinct personalities and moods. Bear societies are organized around a pecking order that develops as bears in an area grow up and learn their relative status through play and fighting. Family groups, especially females with older offspring, are high-ranking.

The years the young spend with their mother represent an intense learning period. The cubs do not realize that their high status is a reflection of their mother's dominance, and they are in for a rude awakening when the spring of their weaning arrives and the female no longer tolerates their presence. On their own for the first time, they are now at the very bottom of the pecking order. Young males almost always leave the area (probably to minimize inbreeding), and females remain where they are raised. These young, curious, insecure bears constantly explore and test their environment and are quick to take advantage of food or garbage left by careless people. Many problem bears are these recently weaned young, which become nuisances to humans and end up being shot.

Below: *Black bears are marginally more successful than their brown relatives, thanks to a slightly higher rate of reproduction and a milder temperament.*

On the conservation front there is cause for both concern and hope. Historically, either black or grizzly bears—or both—inhabited almost every habitat type in North America, while brown bears were found throughout Eurasia. Today, black bears have managed to hold on to more of their original range, though their populations are now more scattered and isolated. Grizzlies have lost 99 percent of their range in the mainland United States.

These small, isolated populations are extremely vulnerable to inbreeding, excessive mortality, and extinction. Only in Alaska, northern Canada, and the former Soviet Union do large tracts of intact grizzly habitat occur. Even in Canada, however, grizzlies have been eliminated from one-quarter of their original range and are considered at risk in 63 percent of their current range. The last strongholds of grizzly and black bears are vulnerable to increasing human populations, uncontrolled resource exploitation, and climatic changes. Poaching of bears to provide the Far East with the prized paws and gallbladders is also a serious problem that continues to worsen.

The long-term conservation of bears will be a difficult and frustrating task. Dedicated biologists risk their lives every year working to gain the knowledge needed to attack the problems. Pay is low, the hours long, and the work dangerous. In spite of this, many scientists are devoting their lives to the cause. They now have the benefits of hindsight from mistakes made elsewhere, as well as recent research data and the advantage of sophisticated techniques. Economic and social pressures, however, often supersede environmental concerns. Nothing is more frustrating than the plight of biologists, handicapped by limited funding and resources, watching bears losing out yet again in the face of human encroachment.

Ideally, we should be providing for the long-term conservation of bears where they

CAUGHT IN THE CROSSFIRE

The European brown bear has disappeared from much of its original range and is highly endangered in many of the areas where small populations still persist. Brown bears probably disappeared from Britain as early as the 10th century. Small remnant populations in France, Italy, and Greece are barely hanging on. Romania, Scandinavia, Poland, Spain, and Czechoslovakia have more secure populations, but there is no reason for complacency.

What was once a success story in the former Yugoslav Republic demonstrates how rapidly conditions can change. The recent outbreak of civil war throughout Croatia and Bosnia-Herzegovina has had tragic human consequences but has also devastated brown bear populations in the area. The war zone includes important national parks where uncontrolled timber exploitation, fires, bombing, and the shooting of wildlife are all taking place. Scientific research has been suspended as a result of the conflict, and income for wildlife management from the sale of hunting licenses has stopped. Djuro Huber, a biologist from Croatia, estimated that as many as two-thirds of Croatia's 250 brown bears could have been killed by the summer of 1992. The spread of fighting to Bosnia and Herzegovina has also resulted in a serious threat to the 800 bears that live there.

are still abundant, rather than waiting until they are scarce. Recent work suggests the need for a series of large protected parks and wilderness areas with adjoining areas suitable for bears. Remnant populations require protection and intense management, and the reintroduction of bears into suitable unoccupied habitat must also be explored. All these steps are necessary to ensure that our children do not inherit a world almost devoid of bears.

As the writer Aldo Leopold said, "relegating grizzlies to Alaska is like relegating happiness to heaven; one may never get there." A country with bears is immeasurably richer. No matter how many times you encounter a bear, it remains a thrilling and humbling experience.

John Hechtel

UNCOMMON SENSES

Above: *The feathery antennae of the male emperor moth enable him to detect a single airborne molecule of a distant female's scent.*

Far right: *Bechstein's bat navigates accurately in the dark by bouncing sound waves off the surface of the water.*

Right: *We describe someone with sharp vision as "eagle-eyed" with good reason— eagles have extremely keen vision. The golden eagle, for example, can spot small mammal prey from high in the air.*

Imagine being able to chart the oceans using the earth's magnetic field; to smell another creature almost half a mile away; to be able to approach it in darkness, yet adapt at once to bright light and see the target underwater from 50 feet away; and then to detect the minute electric fields produced by its muscles. These extraordinary sensory capabilities belong to the blue sharks of the North Atlantic. The female blue shark mates on the east coast of North America, but gives birth 3,000 miles away in the sea off Portugal. On her journey, she is guided day and night by the earth's geomagnetic field —one of the few navigational cues available in an almost featureless sea.

Many other animals possess remarkable sensory abilities. Honed by millions of years of evolution, these faculties ensure that an animal navigates successfully, finds food, and attracts a partner.

The almost miraculous sense of direction possessed by many species has long puzzled naturalists and scientists alike. New evidence suggests that many animals possess a built-in magnetic sense. The key substance is magnetite, an iron-rich mineral that responds to the earth's magnetic field. In animals' bodies, particles of magnetite occur close to bunches of nerve cells. In

bees these particles are located in the abdomen, while in mammals and birds they are concentrated in the nose region. These tiny magnets twist to align themselves with the north or south magnetic poles, producing a torque that the nerve cells pick up. The presence of magnetite enables salamanders to return to their natal ponds, migrating birds to find their way back to their nest sites, sharks and whales to locate feeding and breeding grounds in the vast seas, and tuna to cross oceans on regular routes.

Total reliance on a magnetic sense, however, also results in mass strandings of small whales such as pilot whales. In the middle of the sea, these ocean travelers can swim safely with all their other navigational senses "switched off," guided only by the earth's geomagnetic field lines, or contours. As a result, a pod of whales may follow a magnetic contour over a sandbar or submerged sandy reef and be taken by surprise. The animals activate their other senses, but often it is too late, and they become fatally stranded. Luckily, these strandings are rare.

Perhaps the best-studied navigational marvel is that of bird migration. Here, too, the magnetic sense plays a key role, but birds do not depend on just one guidance system. Those using regular flyways may recognize geographic landmarks such as mountains, lakes, and rivers, while night fliers may listen for biological landmarks such as frogs croaking far below.

Birds generally navigate using the sun, moon, or stars. To use the sun, however, a bird must be able to allow for its changing position. It is possible that by sensing fluctuations in the geomagnetic field, a bird obtains a magnetic map of the world with which it plots a course.

Young migrants inherit, rather than learn, knowledge of the directions in which they

others of its kind by the rate and pattern of the charges they emit.

Electricity is, in fact, produced by all animals—albeit in the tiniest of quantities—when their muscles and nerves are working. Some predators are able to sense this electrical activity and so are led to their next meal. Jelly-filled pits on a shark's snout, known as the *ampullae of Lorenzini,* can even detect the minute electric currents produced by the beating heart of a flatfish. The hammerhead shark has ampullae spread across the front of its broad head, with which it scans the seafloor to find buried fish. The duckbill platypus uses a similar sensor in its snout to probe the river bottom for invertebrates.

Animals have exploited all the available sensory channels to increase their chances of finding food. Pits in the rattlesnake's snout detect the heat given off by prey. The hummingbird can see colors at the ultraviolet end of the light spectrum and follows lines on flower petals, invisible to humans, that guide it to the nectar. The cheetah has a horizontal strip of cells in the back of its eye that focuses the eye on targets silhouetted against the horizon. A "four-eyed" fish has each eye split into two in order to see above and below the water at the same time, while the kingfisher's lens system lets it see well in the air, then change to underwater vision as it dives below the surface. The brown hyena, the wolf, and the red fox all depend on a keen sense of smell to locate prey, while bat-eared foxes, as their name suggests, have extra-large ears with which they listen for termites underground.

Most bats use echolocation to track their airborne insect prey. A cruising bat might produce five or ten sound pulses per second—enough to help it navigate in the dark but insufficient for investigating a target. When it locates prey, however, the bat speeds up the rate to 50 pulses per second; then, as it closes in and needs to know pre-

Above: A formidable hunter, the great white shark depends on its keen sense of smell to find prey. Using nerves concentrated in its nose cone, the great white can detect a single drop of blood diluted in over a million gallons of water.

should go. The westernmost populations of European garden warblers, for example, are programmed to fly southwest in September to head for the Iberian Peninsula, southeast in October to fly from the Straits of Gibraltar to equatorial West Africa, and northeast the following April to return to Europe.

Fish, too, use some remarkable techniques to find their way around. For example, the so-called weak electric fish surround themselves with electrical fields produced by strips of flattened muscles or nerve cells in their tails or the sides of their bodies. By sensing disturbances in this electrical field, a fish can move safely through even the murkiest water and can even recognize

cise details about its target, it increases the number of pulses to over 200 per second.

Some prey species, however, have developed defenses against bat sonar. The tiger moth, for example, can hear a bat's echo-location calls and so take evasive action by flying in loops and plummeting toward the ground. Tropical tiger moths can also jam the bat's sonar. The bat receives an echo from the moth, but just as the bat is diving at maximum speed, the moth fires a burst of sound at it. The bat is startled, and the moth escapes.

Attracting a mate may also involve the use of specialized senses: moths, for example, use an ultradeveloped sense of smell. To attract a mate, the female emits an attractive sex pheromone into the air, which the male can detect diluted down to a single molecule, using the 60,000 sensory hairs of his feathery antennae. Once he has detected about 200 molecules, he tracks the female down and mates with her. The bolas spider has, however, turned this communication system to its advantage. It drops a line of silk ending in a sticky ball and releases chemicals that resemble the pheromones of a female moth. Male moths attracted by the scent are then caught on the whirring lure.

A recent discovery of the natural world is the love call of the African elephant. This call comprises rumbles of such low frequency that they are inaudible to humans.

Because the solitary male may be many miles from a receptive female, and she is ready to mate for only a few days every five years, the female needs to alert a mate to her condition—and low-frequency "infra-sounds" carry farthest.

She calls for about 30 minutes, using the same sequence of repeated patterns. The bull also rumbles in reply, but on reaching the herd, he grows quiet and listens for the female. After mating, she produces a special rumble that sends the rest of the herd into a frenzy. They rumble, trumpet, and defecate in what researchers have called a "mating pandemonium."

For many years a mysterious, deep roar has been heard in the oceans of the world. The pulsed, low-frequency sound was believed to come from a source such as surf crashing on the shore. But investigations have revealed that the sound is produced by the fin whale. Fin whales can be seen traveling alone or in small pods, but these whales are probably part of a much larger herd whose members, perhaps 60 miles apart, communicate with each other using a "sixth sense" that we are only just beginning to understand.

Michael Bright

Left: The hibiscus flower you see here may look very different to a ruby-throated hummingbird, which sees colors that are invisible to the human eye.

Below: Heat-sensitive pits in the bushmaster snake's snout quickly alert it to the presence of warm-blooded prey.

BIRDS OF THE GODS

Right: The Emperor of Germany's bird of paradise displays his impressive tail feathers in a shimmering spectacle of color.

High in the mountains of central New Guinea, the first rays of the rising sun filter through the leafy canopy of the humid, cloud-wrapped forest. Suddenly, a flash of electric blue lights up the somber backdrop of the great trees. The fabulous male blue bird of paradise has arrived at his treetop display site to perform one of the most remarkable courtship rituals in the entire bird kingdom.

At first, he is difficult to distinguish in the gloom of the rainforest, since his body is mainly blackish. Then, in an instant, he swings his body backward to hang upside down from the moss-covered branch. He fans out the spray of shimmering purplish blue feathers, cascading from either side of his breast, to create a psychedelic apron that contrasts startlingly with the spread of velvety black and chestnut red feathers higher on his breast. His two long, wirelike central tail feathers, which are black tipped with blue, encircle his body in a wide arc. Throughout the display, this fantastic creature sings a strange, metallic-sounding rhyth-

mic song, which has been compared both to the noise of an electric drill and that of an alien spacecraft, the sound throbbing in time with the pulsing of the bird's sumptuous plumes.

There are 43 species of birds of paradise, most of which live in the wet forests of New Guinea, with 4 species in eastern Australia and 2 on the Molucca Islands (once known as the Spice Islands) in Indonesia. They range in size from birds little larger than sparrows to some that are as large as magpies. They are all stout—superficially resembling crows or starlings—with rounded wings and large, powerful feet. Most of the species feed mainly on fruit, but the bills of birds of paradise vary greatly, from those that are short and heavy and designed to deal with a varied diet, to the long, slender, downcurved bills of the riflebirds and sicklebills, which are specialized tools for prying out insects from their homes.

However, the most striking feature of this extraordinary family of birds is the stunning plumage of the males. In no other bird family do the males sport such a remarkable range of brilliant ornamental plumage: from breast shields, capes, and cascading flank plumes to long, thin, wirelike feathers extending from the center of the tail or even from the head. The males use this impressive array of finery in ritualized displays at regular sites. Here they parade in splendor to attract the watching females, which are dowdy and inconspicuous by comparison, with mainly brown and gray plumage, often barred underneath.

The display of the male superb bird of paradise is no less stunning than that of the blue bird of paradise. He expands his iridescent green breast shield and spreads his huge, bronze-black cape around his head like some Elizabethan courtier's ruff. As he

Below: The crested bird of paradise inhabits the humid jungles of southeastern New Guinea, along with over 30 other species.

Below: *Found only in the extreme northeast of Australia, the male magnificent riflebird holds a territory year-round. Standing on a branch, he shows off his lustrous breastplate in order to attract females.*

does so, he performs a little dance on his display perch—a large branch in the lower forest canopy—and displays the brilliant yellow inside of his bill as he utters harsh, screaming calls. Another, relatively little-known, species is found only on two islands in the Moluccas group and is known by the name of Wallace's standard-wing. The male of this species raises an iridescent green breast shield, whose feathers are greatly elongated at the sides, so that the shield stands out at right angles to his body. He also raises and lowers a pair of extremely long, narrow white plumes, which extend from the bend of each wing, and erects the feathers on the top of his head.

The male twelve-wired bird of paradise is a stunning black-and-yellow bird with a long bill. Selecting a high, exposed branch for his performance, he erects his black breast shield, which is edged with brilliant emerald green, into a large disk. From his flanks, 12 wire-thin feathers radiate in every direction. Males of this species have also been seen whirling rapidly around a vertical branch, opening and closing their wings in a frenzied performance that is accompanied by sharp metallic calls.

The black sicklebill, a magpie-size bird, erects three pairs of fans from his breast, their deep black feathers scintillating with a violet and green gloss, so that they resemble outstretched arms. The similar-looking brown sicklebill not only gives an equally captivating display but also has an extraordinary call that sounds like a burst of machine-gun fire. The plaintive nasal calls of the ribbon-tailed astrapia, which resemble the croaking of a frog, are less dramatic, but the male makes up for his poor voice with his two astoundingly long white central tail feathers, which can grow to almost four times the length of his body.

Several species of the six-wired bird of paradise of the genus *Parotia* display not high up in the trees but on "courts," which they prepare on the ground, meticulously clearing the area of leaves, twigs, and any other debris. Here, the male performs a ritualized dance, swinging his head about so that the six "wires" that sprout from the sides of his head, each ending in an oval "racket," spin about in all directions.

In contrast to the males of most birds of paradise, which are solitary, those of all but one of the *Paradisaea* species (known as the plumed birds of paradise) display communally. The *Paradisaea* males have huge trains of colorful plumes extending from each side of the breast: red in the Raggiana bird of paradise; red, yellow, and orange with cinnamon tips in the greater bird of paradise; and white and yellow in the Emperor of Germany's bird of paradise. They also have long central tail wires. They display in the treetops in groups of up to 20 birds, extending their wings, raising the flank plumes so that they cascade over the back, and even hanging upside down from the display branch. At their long-established display sites, also known as *arenas* or *leks,* they compete to outperform one another and establish a dominance hierarchy that determines which males mate with the audience of females.

Why is there such a striking difference between the elaborately plumed and gaudy males and the relatively dull females? It is likely that in the first birds of paradise to evolve, the males had much plainer plumage, similar to that of the females, and took only one mate. There are several species alive today, such as the manucodes, the paradigallas, and MacGregor's bird of paradise, that are still like this. However, in much of the lush New Guinea rainforest, food—especially fruit—is so plentiful that the female rarely needs the male to help her find and gather it. Released from this duty, the males were able to spend much of their time and energy on their courtship displays, which enabled them to mate with more than one female. Since these polygamous males produced more young than the monogamous males, their genes were transmitted to more chicks and there was a gradual tendency within the family for the males to evolve ever more elaborate and colorful display plumage.

Another reason for the development of this spectacular plumage may have been the absence of native predators on New

Guinea, which enabled the male birds to display boldly without the fear of being snapped up. Today, however, birds of paradise are at risk—from people. But traditional hunting of birds of paradise by the indigenous population of New Guinea appears to have had relatively little effect on the numbers of most of the species, since hunting was for many years essentially self-regulated at sustainable levels. As is the

Above: *Slightly smaller than a starling, the king bird of paradise is the smallest member of the bird of paradise family.*

Above: *Wilson's bird of paradise has distinctive vivid blue patches of bare skin on the crown.*

Above right: *The crested bird of paradise is the only species that builds a spherical roofed nest close to the ground.*

and the blue bird of paradise, are starting to decline. Few of the polygamous species suffer unduly from hunting because the males, which take no part in caring for the offspring, take up to 10 years to become sexually mature and acquire their gorgeous plumes. So if a mature male is killed, there are plenty of young males ready to take his place. By contrast, monogamous species, such as MacGregor's bird of paradise (which, although lacking dramatic plumes, is often hunted for food), share the task of feeding and rearing the young, and their populations are therefore extremely susceptible to hunting pressure.

However, the hunting by indigenous populations pales into insignificance when compared to the heedless plunder of birds of paradise by 19th-century European settlers. In order to supply the colonial plume trade and decorate ladies' hats and garments, approximately 80,000 skins were exported each year from New Guinea to Europe and North America. The number was probably even higher in some years; 30,000 skins were sold in London alone in 1913. At the turn of the century, one German animal dealer considered the blue bird of paradise so beautiful that he dedicated it to the crown prince of Austria. Skins from this exotic-looking creature may have sold for as much as $200 each.

Fortunately, there was a great reaction against this sickening, wholesale slaughter in Europe, and the antiplume trade movement in Britain produced what was to become the Royal Society for the Protection of Birds. By 1910 the British Parliament had passed a bill that prohibited the sale or exchange of bird of paradise plumes. In 1913 the United States government banned the importation of all bird plumage, and Britain, Canada, and Australia, together with the other Commonwealth colonies, soon followed suit. The demise of the plumage trade was further hastened by the outright banning of

case with many other wildlife conservation issues, the conservation of birds of paradise is intimately bound up with the needs and rights of local peoples.

The adoption, however, by tribal people of modern weapons in place of their traditional bows and arrows has led to the killing of more birds—not just for their plumes but also for food. As a result, some of the scarcer species, such as the black sicklebill

the commercial killing of the birds in New Guinea by the Dutch in 1924.

Today, birds of paradise face the increasing—and far more serious—threat of habitat destruction. At present, the threat has yet to take effect for many species, since New Guinea is one country where large areas of relatively undisturbed rainforest remain. But for how long will these areas be intact? Already farmers have taken over considerable amounts of land, and the blue bird of paradise, for instance, which needs large tracts of undisturbed forest, is losing its habitat. At lower altitudes, it may also suffer from competition with the Raggiana bird of paradise, which can adapt to a wider range of habitats.

Let us hope that these worrisome trends can be reversed and that the conservation programs now under way in New Guinea will preserve much of its pristine rainforest, so that the fabulous birds of paradise they contain will remain for future generations to marvel at.

Jonathan Elphick

CREATURES OF MYTH & SPLENDOR

Birds of paradise have long been known to the tribal people of New Guinea, who use the males' ornamental feathers for ceremonial purposes, especially in elaborate headdresses, and as currency (for example, as wedding gifts). However, the birds were virtually unknown in the West until the early 17th century, when explorers and merchants began shipping the feathers to Europe. The explorers did not see the living birds, and the skins they acquired had the wings and legs cut off to show off the gorgeous plumes to the best advantage. In addition, the birds were known by the people of the Molucca Islands as the "birds of the gods." All of these facts combined led to the belief that birds of paradise spent their entire lives in the air, feeding on air and dew,

with no need for legs. It was even thought that the females incubated their eggs in hollows on the backs of the males as they flew along.

By the beginning of the 19th century, the truth about these amazing birds was gradually coming to light. The first naturalist to see them alive, in 1824, was the Frenchman René Lesson. Other naturalists followed soon afterward, including Alfred Wallace, the great English naturalist and coproposer with Darwin of the theory of evolution. Wallace described several species and was the first to send accurate reports of the male birds' unusual displays. The first photographs of the birds displaying in the wild were not taken until 1957. Even today, details of the lives of some species are barely known.

WHALE WATCHING

Above: *Some gray whales have started to respond positively to researchers, approaching their boats and soliciting attention from them. Other grays, however, go out of their way to avoid humans.*

Right: *The gray whale is the most primitive of all the living whales. It has remained virtually unchanged for millions of years, yet it has one of the largest and most sophisticated brains of any living animal.*

The California gray whale has proved itself to be one of the most astonishingly resilient of the world's animals. Twice in the past 150 years the species has been hunted to near extinction, yet its recovery to preexploitation levels now seems to be assured. The history of the California gray is more closely linked to humans than that of any other whale, so it is especially heartening that there are grounds for optimism about its revival.

The California gray whale population was 22,000 to 23,000 as of spring 1992, and it has been increasing at a rate of just over three percent a year. The main limitation on population growth seems to be the capacity of the animals' Arctic feeding grounds to support them. This area can probably sustain 24,000 gray whales—more than the number that now migrate there in summer.

A yearly journey of 12,500 miles dominates a gray whale's life. It feeds during the summer in the Bering, Chukchi, and Beaufort seas in the Arctic, then swims to the warm, protected waters of a few isolated lagoons in Baja California to mate and bear its young in winter. The return migration to the Arctic begins in mid-February. Newly pregnant females leave first, followed by the males. Mothers with new offspring are the last to leave, sometimes remaining until late spring or early summer. By the end of March, the whale population in the lagoons is at an annual low.

With the exception of mother-calf pairs, gray whales migrate independently. However, because they follow a narrow route along the coast, they may give the impression of mass migration. Swimming along

ern European whalers were sailing the oceans to find these floating fortunes. In the 1840s whalers discovered the California gray whale's coastal migration and set up whaling stations along its route.

A few years afterward the California gray whale was thought to be extinct, and the whaling stations closed. The reprieve was brief, however. Early in this century the combination of steam-powered whalers and exploding harpoon guns made gray whale hunting a lucrative business once again. The partly rejuvenated stock, numbering some 15,000 or more animals, once more came under attack.

After the second onslaught against them, the population of California gray whales was reduced to less than 3,000, yet they continued to be hunted. Finally, in 1946, the newly formed International Whaling Commission (IWC) ratified the International Convention for the Regulation of Whaling. The new treaty prohibited killing of gray whales except by indigenous peoples or by contracting governments when the products were for the use of such peoples. The regulations have been effective on the whole.

The coastal migration and concentrated wintering grounds that once made the California gray whale susceptible to exploitation are now working to its advantage. The species' high reproductive rate, lack of natural predators, low mortality rate, and fairly uncompromised food source have all permitted a recovery that seems miraculous. It has been so successful that in 1978 the

Below: *The blow is a spectacular sight. From a distance, it may be the only indication of a gray whale's presence.*

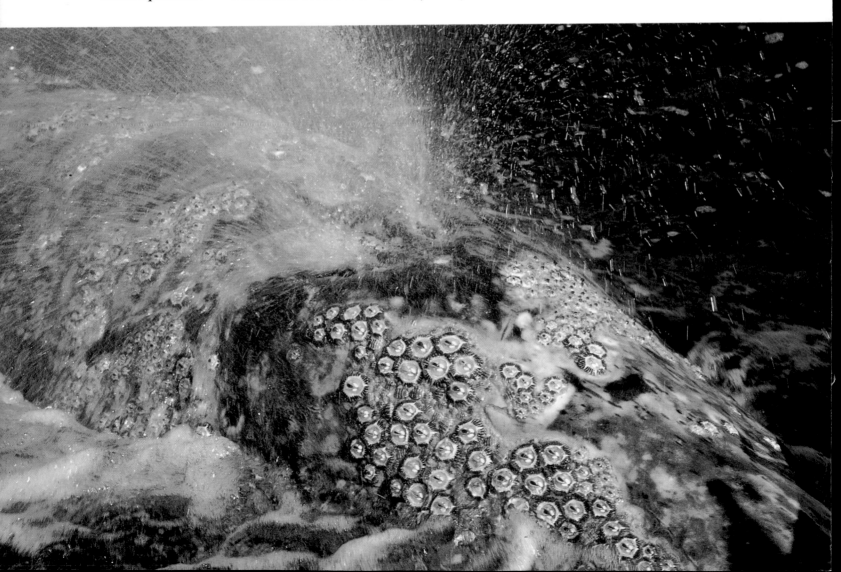

U.S. National Marine Fisheries Service downlisted the California stock from endangered to sustained management status. In 1991 the Service began proceedings to have it delisted altogether.

Today, whale watching replaces whale killing as a significant industry. Along the west coast of North America people pay to see living whales—to marvel at the magnificence of these giant sea creatures. Nevertheless, some threats remain.

A migrating gray whale may run into the gill nets that commercial fisheries use along the Pacific coast. In 1988 gill nets were outlawed along much of the California coast, but some are still in use, and whales occasionally die as a result of entanglement.

The IWC also continues to set noncommercial quotas, and in recent years whalers from the former Soviet Union killed 167 gray whales annually in the name of their indigenous peoples. Despite recent political changes in this region, it is likely that this killing will continue.

With the spread of seismic exploration for gas and oil reserves, some migrating gray whales now avoid exploration areas.

Even more serious is the fact that some grays have abandoned affected feeding and wintering grounds. This situation may be threatening if Mexico decides to exploit reserves in the mating and calving lagoons. The United States and Canada are also increasing oil and gas exploration and production in the feeding areas. A major oil spill in feeding or calving areas could have a disastrous effect on the gray whales. Statistically, the U.S. government considers this risk minimal, but the *Exxon Valdez* disaster gives reason to question this assessment.

Despite anxiety about these potential dangers, the reality is that the California gray whale's recovery at the beginning of the 1990s is nothing less than spectacular. As we increase knowledge and understanding of the gray whale and its revival, the lessons learned may aid the recovery of other species. We may also hope that by taking time to watch these whales, we will come to appreciate the benefits of being surrounded by such awesome and beautiful creatures and therefore find it easier to temper our appetites so as not to endanger them again.

Jeff Hall

Below: *When migrating, the gray whale stays in waters less than 650 feet deep. An expert at navigating in relatively shallow water, it is stranded far less often than other species.*

FLYING INTO TROUBLE

Above: *An exhausted crossbill takes a much-needed rest after a long and arduous migration.*

Right: *After spending the winter months in South Africa, swallows begin to gather in flocks in preparation for their spring flight north.*

Below: *In Hungary, 2,500 artificial nest platforms have been built for the white stork.*

There are few more awe-inspiring feats in the natural world than the journeys made by migratory birds. These tiny scraps of life make annual journeys over deserts, mountains, and oceans between their breeding quarters in the northern hemisphere and their tropical winter homes. Each year, some five billion land birds travel from Europe and northern Asia to Africa, braving natural hazards from storms and starvation to birds of prey.

These natural threats have little impact on the huge flocks involved, but increasingly the migrants are having to cope with changes in the environment brought about by rising human populations. They face the loss of forests, wetlands, and grasslands, as well as the effects of pollutants, collisions with man-made structures, and hunting.

It is becoming ever more urgent to discover more about migrants' needs. This is vital not only to help save the birds, but also because migrants serve as early indicators of impending environmental disasters.

A striking example of this began back in the late 1960s and involved a little warbler known as the whitethroat. Analysis of the Common Birds Census in Britain for the year 1969 showed a sudden dearth of this migrant in its hedgerow nesting habitat—numbers had slumped by a staggering 71 percent between 1968 and 1969. The trend was mirrored across western Europe.

The cause was traced to the savanna and grasslands of Africa's western Sahel region on the southern borders of the Sahara, where the warblers spend the winter. In the summer of 1968 the rains failed, and the resulting drought, intensified by desertification, wiped out many of the whitethroats. Numbers have remained low ever since, although there has been a recent increase due to improved rainfall in the Sahel.

It is not just songbirds that are affected by events in Africa. The white stork is in trouble both in its African wintering quarters and in its European breeding range. The combined effects of drought in the Sudan and the Sahel and irrigation projects deprive the storks of their wet grassland feeding sites. Locust eradication in West Africa has also depleted a major food source.

When the storks fly north in spring to breed in Europe, they arrive in a landscape that has undergone radical changes over the past 40 years. Wet meadows and rough pastures have been drained and plowed to grow high-yield crops, greatly reducing the numbers of the storks' prey such as voles, frogs, and grasshoppers.

In Sweden, Denmark, Germany, Austria, and Switzerland, about 80 percent of storks have been lost since 1900. The casualties in Spain have been particularly high. The birds are also faring poorly in eastern Europe, as a result of damage caused by agricultural changes and pollution.

Above: *The Dalmatian pelican is one of many migrant species shot purely for sport in the Mediterranean region.*

Traditional nest sites on buildings are disappearing: new roof designs do not suit the storks' bulky stick nests, and repair work on church steeples and electricity towers destroys nests or causes birds to leave. Overhead cables kill many of these large birds, especially the inexperienced young.

About 6,000 storks are shot each year by hunters as the birds pass through Syria and Lebanon, affecting populations breeding in eastern Europe and southwest Asia. Some 2,000 to 3,000 eastern white storks die in other wintering areas. Several thousand of the storks breeding in western Europe are killed during migration and in winter, mainly in the Niger wetlands and in northern Nigeria.

The slaughter of migrant birds is rife in many Mediterranean countries. About ten million hunters and a million trappers kill an estimated one billion birds annually, ranging from tiny warblers to pelicans and eagles. Heavy hunting in restricted areas such as islands, small estuaries, and marshes not only kills many birds but also disturbs the other birds in the area. This can have serious implications if the site is a crucial stopover point for long-distance migrants.

Wetland migratory birds are especially at risk from habitat destruction. Cranes, geese, and waders gather in enormous numbers to pause for rest and food at relatively few stopover sites. Almost the entire Pacific coast

populations of western sandpipers and dunlins rely on the stopover site at the Copper River Delta in southeast Alaska, while some 80 percent of red knots migrating along the east coast of the United States depend on the rich harvest of horseshoe crab eggs in the Delaware Bay. Red knots and sanderlings are diminishing, with resort development and beach erosion threatening areas of the Delaware Bay and oil spills jeopardizing other vital points on their route. Oil pollution also afflicts seabirds on their long ocean wanderings. In addition, fishing robs them of their food and leaves deadly snares in the form of loose sections of netting.

North American migrant songbirds are essentially tropical species that spend the spring and summer up north, where they are able to exploit the seasonal bounty of insect food. They need extensive tracts of mature forest in both northern and southern habitats. The yellow-throated vireo, Acadian flycatcher, Swainson's warbler, hooded warbler, wood thrush, and American redstart are all declining alarmingly. Their northern breeding forests are being cleared for lumber, agriculture, or development, and the fragmented remnants are less suitable for breeding. The cleared areas attract nest predators such as blue jays, raccoons, and cats, as well as cowbirds, which, like cuckoos, lay their eggs in songbirds' nests at the host family's expense.

The North American migrants are also losing their tropical forest winter habitat, as the rapidly growing human population satisfies its needs for living space, food, fuel, and work. The countries worst hit include Jamaica and the Dominican Republic, and there is virtually no natural forest left in Haiti and El Salvador. Cuba, Guatemala, and Honduras are not far behind. In Costa Rica the remaining tropical forests will disappear within 30 years at present rates of destruction—and the birds with them.

Although a great deal of time and effort

are put into banding, radio-tagging, site censuses, and other research on migratory birds, we still know far too little. Protection of migrants is especially complex because many different habitats and countries may be involved, requiring detailed programs of research and conservation. But it is vital to learn from the birds themselves and transcend national boundaries to coordinate protection measures, or many of our best-loved and most familiar migrant birds will some day leave our shores never to return.

Jonathan Elphick

Above: *Barnacle geese rely on a few specific stopover points where they can recuperate during migration.*

Below: *The tiny Cape May warbler heads north each spring from the West Indies to the northern United States and Canada. This epic journey can total more than 3,000 miles.*

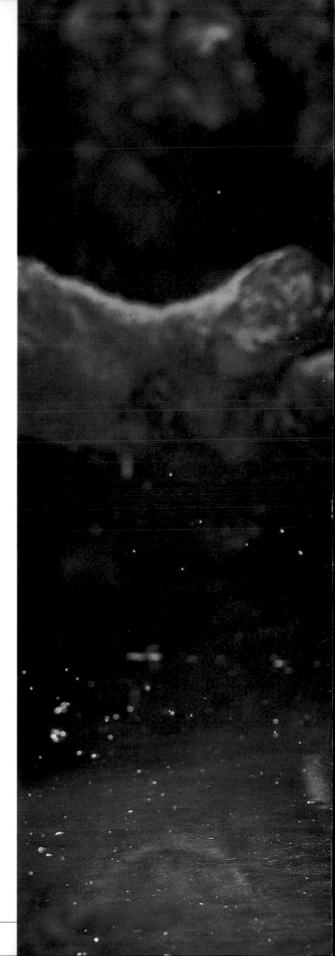

ANIMALS IN MOTION

Above: *The long and muscular hind legs of the grasshopper enable it to leap high in relation to its size. The source of its power is a rubbery protein called* **resilin.**

Right: *The basilisk lizard derives its alternative name of Jesus lizard from its apparent ability to walk on water. In fact, it must run in order to stay on the surface, and can only manage this feat over short distances.*

From the fluttering butterfly to the bounding kangaroo, all animals are to some extent defined by the way they move. The ability to move—whether a few inches or from one end of the earth to the other—enables animals to find food, hunt prey, escape predators, seek mates, colonize new areas, and take shelter.

Since water comprises the largest habitat on earth, it is not surprising that an enormous diversity of species move by swimming. For microscopic creatures, water is sticky, and they require a lot of power to move through it. Many of these tiny animals have flagella—tiny, hairlike structures that beat with a wavelike motion to push the water backward and sideways.

Some small organisms, such as the larvae of many marine snails, worms, and starfish, have bands of shorter hairs called *cilia*. Each cilium straightens as it beats against the water, then bends on the return stroke, offering minimal resistance to the water.

Larger and faster animals rely on muscles for movement. Muscles are made of proteins that stretch and contract. In its resting position, a muscle is usually fully extended, and it needs energy to contract.

Simple, soft-bodied animals such as flatworms and sea hares bend their bodies by contracting certain muscles while relaxing others. They swim with graceful undulations. The hydra uses muscles to bend to one side, shrink and extend its body, and wave its tentacles.

Opposing sets of muscles are used for more complex movements. The earthworm has bands of circular muscles around its body, which squeeze it into a long, thin

shape, while contracting strips of longitudinal muscles make it short and fat. Tiny bristles, called *chaetae*, on its underside anchor the worm on irregularities in the soil as it pulls its body forward. A jellyfish propels itself through the water by jet propulsion. As circular muscles in its bell contract, water shoots out backward and propels the animal forward.

For more powerful and effective locomotion, the muscles need something rigid against which to work. The arthropods—the crustaceans, insects, and their relatives—have an exoskeleton, or rigid outer shell. They were probably the first animals to have specialized limbs for swimming and walking. In arthropods, the exoskeleton is jointed to allow complex movements.

In arthropod limbs, pairs of muscles are attached across the joints to work in opposite directions. This process, in which one muscle contracts to bend the limb and the other straightens it, is also found in the more advanced vertebrates.

The evolution of muscle blocks pulling against rigid bones enabled early fish to move fast and become successful predators. Most fish swim by flexing their bodies, fins, and tails in wavelike motions to displace water. The fins are used for steering, braking, stabilizing, and propulsion. Only a few species, such as the boxfish and the seahorse, are so heavily armored that they rely entirely on their fins for movement.

The streamlined body of a typical fish reduces its drag, and overlapping scales, thickly coated in mucus, also help cut down resistance. The greatest streamlining is found in fast-swimming fish like tuna and mackerel, but the speed record is held by the oceangoing sailfish, which can swim at up to 70 miles per hour in short bursts.

buoyancy. In some primitive species the swim bladder connects to the mouth and probably evolved from a rudimentary lung, but in most the bladder is self-contained, and the gas is produced by chemical processes. The fish produces or reabsorbs gas to adjust its density as it changes depth.

Movement on land presents a whole new set of challenges. The drag created by friction with the ground makes it advantageous to lift the body above the surface, but for this, gravity must be overcome and the body's weight must be supported by strong limbs.

The key to walking and running is balance. Arthropods, with many legs and bodies close to the ground, have little problem. However, with four legs, balance requires great control. For a dog, walking is easy, but as it speeds up, only two legs are on the ground at a time. If it gallops, it may have only one leg on the ground at any one time, or it may even have all four legs off the ground. The dog maintains balance because its steps follow each other so quickly.

Below: *Although its anatomy seems crudely adapted for movement, the southern stingray can "fly" through the water, propelled by its winglike fins.*

The legs of marine mammals have become modified to form flippers or paddles and, in the case of whales and dolphins, are assisted by muscular tail flukes. Whales, dolphins, and many seals undulate their bodies up and down instead of from side to side as they swim.

Since all living matter is denser than water, swimming animals must achieve buoyancy. Microscopic floating organisms have long spines to increase their surface area-to-volume ratio, but in mobile animals this would increase drag. Some animals avoid sinking by swimming all the time. Water beetles trap a "float" of air under bristles on their bellies, and some sea slugs gulp air at the surface. Squid, sharks, and a few other fish use lateral fins to generate lift, but they need to keep moving or else they sink.

Most fish, however, have a gas-filled swim bladder, which contains gas that alters their

Above: *The impala's bounding run helps it escape from predators. By leaping high, it is able to reduce its contact with the ground and thereby minimize friction, which would slow it down.*

Tendons greatly enhance the thrust of limb against ground. Made of elastic material, they attach muscle firmly to bone. The Achilles tendon at the back of the heel is particularly important to mammals. As the foot touches down, the muscle and tendon relax, storing energy. The energy is released, springlike, as the foot pushes off from the ground. Kangaroos and horses have particularly powerful tendons, which also cushion the impact of landing at speed. The storage of energy in elastic material is also the secret of the flea's jump, the grasshopper's leap, and the power of insect flight.

Fast-moving animals such as gazelles and cheetahs have long legs to help thrust themselves off the ground for longer periods, reducing friction. The cheetah also has a very flexible spine, enabling it to swing its hind legs forward in front of its forelegs while galloping at speeds of up to 60 miles an hour.

Perhaps the strangest skeletal adaptation is that of the snakes, which have evolved without limbs. Most snakes rely on friction against the ground in order to move, and to achieve this they throw the body into a series of curves. On the outer part of the curve, the body presses against irregularities in the ground, much as an eel pushes

Right: *The boa's sinuous movement is the result of friction between the snake's body and the surface it moves over.*

against the water to obtain thrust. This method also works in underground tunnels, and some snakes use a similar technique to climb trees, pressing against ridges in the bark. A few species of snake, such as the puff adder, travel forward in a straight line. They have specially hinged scales that can be raised and lowered by muscles to push against bumps in the ground.

Some animals have developed the ability to leave the ground completely and move through the air. However, true flight is a complex process. Bats have membranes of skin stretched between greatly elongated fingers, and their wrist bones are fused to provide strong anchorage for the muscles. But they lack the tail feathers of birds, which are useful in braking and turning.

In cross section a bird's wing has a concave lower surface, and its curved leading edge tapers to a thinner trailing edge. In flight, air passing over the wing travels farther than air below it. It therefore travels faster, reducing pressure above the wing. The opposite happens below the wing, and this pressure difference generates lift.

The downbeat of the wing presses down and back against the air, with the feathers spread to create the largest possible surface. On the upbeat the wing is folded slightly, and the feathers are compressed to minimize drag. Each of the main flight feathers can twist slightly, so that the wing is, in effect, made up of a series of small propellers that further aid flight. The body feathers streamline the bird's outline, while the tail feathers can serve as a rudder or a brake.

At low speeds, turbulence is a problem, especially around the edges of the wing. To combat this, slow-flying or gliding birds can usually part the primary feathers to form slots that allow air to pass through. And by flying in V-shaped flocks, migrating geese may exploit each other's slipstreams.

To avoid stalling on landing, a bird brings its alula, or bastard wing, into play. This

works a little like the flaps of an airplane. The sight of pigeons spreading their tail feathers and angling their wings in order to brake is familiar to anyone who has watched pigeons landing on a city street. A similar technique is used by hovering birds such as kestrels to reduce their forward thrust.

The true hoverers are the hummingbirds, whose wings describe a figure eight, which allows them to remain in the same position as they feed from flowers. They are the only birds that can fly forward and backward. Some hummingbirds can beat their wings up to 50 times a second. Their high-sugar nectar food provides the energy necessary for such a strenuous lifestyle.

Birds use many techniques to save energy while flying. Small birds often have a dipping flight, flapping their wings to generate momentum, then gliding down briefly before the next flap. Many large birds seek out rising air currents, or thermals, and spiral upward on them, wings spread wide. They

Above: *This sequence of a leafhopper taking off shows how the insect streamlines its body in order to reduce drag in the initial stages. Once it is airborne, wing power takes over.*

may rise to heights of over 6,500 feet before coasting down, often traveling several miles without having to flap their wings. Seabirds also make use of the rising air currents that are found as the onshore wind sweeps over cliffs and headlands. Soaring birds such as vultures and eagles usually have long, strong wings, with widespread primary feathers to give added lift.

Swooping and diving require the opposite approach: the body must fall through the air like a stone. The peregrine falcon folds its wings close to its body as it plunges earth-ward, and there are claims that stooping peregrines have reached speeds of almost 220 miles per hour. Brown pelicans, boobies, and gannets assume a similar shape as they plunge into the waves.

Insects have flown for some 200 million years. Most adult insects have two pairs of wings attached to the thorax, although in the beetles one pair has hardened into elytra, or wing covers. The oldest flying insects are the dragonflies, and they are remarkable in that their two pairs of wings can operate quite independently of each other. Each

Right: *The dormouse's body is not well adapted for leaping, since it has weak legs and a heavy torso. However, it is capable of jumping if absolutely necessary.*

Left: *As a member of the beetle family, the ladybug has only one pair of wings. The other pair evolved into elytra, cases that cover the functional wings when the insect is not in flight.*

wing moves at an angle to the body, first downward and forward, then upward and backward. This helps to reduce drag and increase lift.

The wings of dragonflies, locusts, and butterflies are attached to the thorax through slots in its sides. The main flight muscles join the bottom of the thorax. The wings pivot on the thorax wall, acting as levers that produce a large wing movement for a relatively small muscle contraction initiated by a nerve impulse.

Dragonfly wings beat at about 20 beats a second. This is slow by insect standards—bees flap their wings 180 times a second, and mosquitoes 600 times a second. Such rapid wing beats cannot be triggered by individual nerve impulses. Instead, faster wing beats use a different action. The wings are attached directly to the thorax, and the flight muscles are attached to the top and bottom of the thorax. As the flight muscles contract and relax, the wings are moved up and down. These muscles are a special type that can produce about 40 wing beats for every nerve impulse. These wing beats also make use of the sudden release of energy stored in the rubbery protein resilin, just as in the case of the jumping flea.

The immense diversity of animal locomotion calls for a great input of sensory information to each animal's brain. Height,

Left: *The widely spread outer flight feathers of the white-backed vulture help it to soar on air currents for hours with little muscular effort. This is essential to its habit of scavenging carrion, which it spots from high in the air.*

speed, direction, balance, and the various limbs all must be coordinated, and the brain has to interpret the changing scene viewed by the eyes. In more advanced animals, subtle control of movement involves information from stretch sensors in the muscles and the movements of fluid in the semicircular canals of the vertebrate ear, which maintain stability and achieve movement. Hand in hand with the development of such complexity has gone evolution itself. As a result of being able to move from one place to another, animals from widely separated locations are able to come together to mate and breed, thus enhancing genetic variation and the potential for further evolutionary changes.

Jill Bailey

A BIRD IN THE HAND

Right: *Falconry has an international history, spanning thousands of years. It has long been popular among Muslim peoples, and the sport is mentioned in the Koran.*

Falconry is a sport with a rich and fascinating history. Although it declined in the 19th century, it regained popularity after World War II and is now flourishing among dedicated followers throughout the world. In addition to providing recreation for those who practice it, falconry has played an important role in conserving certain endangered species of birds of prey.

The first depictions of people with large birds on their wrists come from the Far East, on materials dated around 2000 B.C. The sport has a long tradition in Great Britain, and in medieval times falconry enjoyed the popularity that a sport such as soccer has today. *The Boke of St. Albans* prescribed the types of bird suitable for those in different walks of life, such as the gyrfalcon (for royalty) and the goshawk (for a yeoman). Soldiers returning from the Crusades brought home new training techniques from the Middle East, where hawking had been popular for many centuries. The prominence falconry once had in British life is reflected in the number of words it has given to the language. The word *hawker,* meaning "peddler," is just one of many words that have their origin in falconry.

Traditionally, falconers divide the birds they fly into three groups: longwings, shortwings, and broadwings. Each differs in temperament, shape, and style of hunting. The longwings are the true falcons of the genus *Falco.* They have relatively long, narrow wings that come to a point and a bill that has a notch in the upper edge, which delivers a fatal bite.

Longwings are comparatively placid and easy to tame. The kestrel is a popular spe-

Above: *Eagles are not generally trained for falconry, since they are heavy birds to carry on the fist. However, their soaring flight makes them attractive to some specialists.*

cies for beginners, while the merlin was once considered a "ladies' bird." The larger falcons, such as the peregrine, are capable of breathtaking flights. They may "mount" to a "pitch" of 330 to 985 feet, then "stoop" on grouse or partridge that has been flushed by the falconer or his dog. Other large falcons, like sakers and gyrfalcons, are not so suitable for this kind of flight, since they often take prey by attacking it on the ground.

Falconers refer to all trained birds of prey as hawks, which can be confusing. True hawks of the genus *Accipiter* are known as shortwings. Typical shortwings, such as

goshawks and sharp-shins, have shorter and wider wings than falcons. These, combined with their long tails, give them great agility in the air. In the wild, shortwings hunt mainly from perches, so trained birds are often slipped straight from their trainer's fist to dash and weave after prey as it twists through cover. A shortwing may crash into a bush to seize a rabbit or pheasant with its relatively long legs, delivering the death blow with its talons. These birds are not for beginners, since they are not easily tamed, or "manned," and they remain rather temperamental despite training.

Eagles, buzzards, and related species have even deeper wings—thus, their collective name of broadwings. These wings fit them for soaring flight. The Harris' hawks and red-tailed hawks of North America are really buzzards, but they can be skillful hunters and have become popular among falconers. Most eagles are too heavy to be popular. As a group, broadwings are more placid than the true hawks. They are quite easy to breed in enclosures and can take birds from pheasants to small waterfowl, and mammals from hares to squirrels.

A trained hawk takes less prey than a wild hawk or even a domestic cat in the country. Furthermore, a gun provides more game for the table, so it is not surprising that falconry declined in Europe when guns became more reliable. Nevertheless, a succession of small clubs kept the skills alive both in Great Britain and the United States. Falconry clubs were reestablished in other European countries during the first half of the 20th century. During the 1960s there was something of a falconry renaissance, perhaps stimulated by the growing general interest in wildlife.

Today, there are more than a thousand falconers in Britain, Germany, and the United States, with several hundred more throughout western Europe, Canada, New Zealand, and southern Africa. There are probably at least as many again in Middle Eastern countries, Turkey, the Indian subcontinent, and southern parts of the former Soviet Union. Many clubs make contact and cooperate with each other through the International Association of Falconry and the Convention on Conservation of Birds of Prey.

Before World War II, few birds of prey were protected by law. Falconers traditionally took birds from nests, as "eyasses" (nestlings) or trapped them in their first fall as "passagers." Adult raptors are long-lived, and most species used in falconry have between two and four young in a nest each

year. This surplus meant that many trained hawks were traditionally "hacked back" to the wild. Other hawks simply returned to the wild after being lost while hunting. In Britain, goshawks were released to reestablish a wild stock that had become extinct in the 19th century.

Today, Eastern falconers continue to trap and release hawks, as they have for centuries. In the West, however, falconry practices have been radically affected by the farm chemicals that almost wiped out some raptor populations in the 1950s and 1960s. The insecticide DDT stopped peregrines from breeding successfully, and dieldrin killed many birds. As a result, Western falconers were no longer permitted to take hawks from the wild without a license, just as interest in falconry was starting up again.

These restrictions led to high prices being offered for birds of prey and to some birds being taken without licenses. In Denmark, where DDT had almost wiped out the en-

Above: *This falconer is wearing a "cadge"—a frame that supports several hawks.*

Left: *A hood prevents the kestrel from spotting prey and becoming agitated before the falconer releases it from the fist.*

records began, and falconers have helped in many wild bird studies.

Today, British falconers must breed their own birds, and they are required to have a license for every bird. Very few licenses are given for wild birds of prey, and only a few wild hawks and falcons are taken illegally—with harsh penalties for the poachers when they are caught. Raptors whose populations have been declining in Britain, such as harriers and barn owls, are not used at all for falconry. The British example demonstrates that, with proper controls, raptor populations are able to thrive alongside large numbers of falconers. There is still considerable debate, however, over whether falconers contribute effectively to raptor conservation if the birds are kept separate from wild populations.

Above: *This peregrine falcon is launched in pursuit of grouse in the north of England. Peregrine populations were reestablished in other countries by falconers.*

tire peregrine population, ruthless hawk dealers took young from the last surviving pair of these birds. In view of such behavior, it is hardly surprising that bird protectors started campaigns to ban falconry.

Yet despite condemnation from conservationists during the pesticide era, many falconers started applying the knowledge they had acquired through the sport to conservation projects. The restriction on wild birds led falconers to breed birds of prey in enclosures. This had previously been thought impossible, but enough birds were bred under these conditions for release programs to be initiated. Falconers such as Professors Tom Cade and Christian Saar knew the best conditions in which to release raptors and ensure their survival in the wild and were responsible for reestablishing peregrines in parts of North America and Germany. Falconers have also run a successful project to save the Mauritius kestrel, and species that they are currently helping to rescue include the California condor and the Philippine eagle. In Britain, the wild peregrine population is now higher than at any time since

Right: *Broadwings like the common buzzard are trained to pursue prey that varies from pheasants to squirrels.*

Countries such as the United States and Zimbabwe have another approach. Those who qualify for a falconry license are permitted one or two wild birds a year, of a species that is abundant. In these countries, falconers still do much of the fieldwork on wild birds of prey.

After a difficult period, falconers are becoming accepted again among conservationists. Unfortunately, birds of prey remain at risk in many parts of the world. Damaging pesticides are still used in developing countries, and habitat loss is the most serious threat of all. Raptor stocks can recover from pollution and persecution if steps are taken in time. This is the challenge that falconers have the skills to meet: helping raptors survive in the future.

Dr. R. E. Kenward

TRAINING A BIRD OF PREY

Training a bird of prey can be divided into three stages. First is the manning process, during which the hawk learns to trust the falconer and then becomes accustomed to the other sights and sounds of the world of humans. The falconer makes all the introductions gradually, while the bird feeds on the fist.

In the "calling off" stage, the hawk learns to fly to the fist for food. A light line, the creance, is initially attached to leather straps, known as jesses, on the hawk's legs. The lure, a token prey with meat attached, is also introduced at this stage. The falconer later swings the lure in the air for free-flying longwings to chase, as a way of improving their flight skills.

In the third stage, the hawk is "entered"—released to fly after suitable quarry. In the past, hawks were equipped only with jesses and a specially resonant bell that could be heard from hundreds of feet away. Hawks today are flown with tiny radio transmitters, so that they can be found more easily when they fly out of sight. For a longwing, a hood is also important to prevent the bird from seeing prey before the falconer is ready to release it. Once the bird makes a kill, it may then be picked up or "called down" to the fist or lure for food.

The key to success in all stages of training is the feeding regime. A hawk is trained when it is most receptive—such as when it is eager for its daily meal. It must not be kept short of food, however, or it will lack stamina for long flights, and its health could suffer.

WINGS OVER THE DINOSAUR WORLD

Right: *Over a thousand pterosaur specimens have been found to date. This example, discovered over 200 years ago in Bavaria, is one of the finest and most complete.*

I hold in my fingers the impression of a small, delicate skeleton, its neck arched, wings and legs jumbled together, and jaws agape, just as it came to rest on the seafloor 150 million years ago. This is all that remains of a pterosaur (often referred to as a pterodactyl)—arguably one of the most extraordinary creatures ever to have existed. The animal now trapped in this extremely rare fossil once swooped over a world filled with reptiles. On land, herds of plant-eating dinosaurs such as stegosaurs were trailed by flesh eaters such as the fleet-footed dromaeosaurs. The seas were hunting grounds for ichthyosaurs (dolphinlike fish catchers) and the huge predatory plesiosaurs. Over them all flew pterosaurs, the first true vertebrate fliers.

Following a massive meteorite impact, a radical change in the climate, or some other cataclysmic event, the pterosaurs, dinosaurs, and other groups died out about 65 million years ago. So all that we know about pterosaurs has been deduced from their fossil remains. Usually only the hardest tissues, such as bone, are preserved. But the shape and relative size of fossil bones reveal a great deal about basic pterosaur anatomy: they tell us how the joints worked and suggest the muscles that controlled them. Internal casts of the braincase and, on very rare occasions, the almost miraculous preservation of soft tissues have also provided valuable insights into the nature of the brain, wing structure, and body covering. The age and geographic distribution of finds, kinds of sediment in which the remains are preserved, and even the "death pose" of the skeleton are all further grist for the paleontologist's mill.

The first and one of the best pterosaur specimens came to light in Bavaria in 1784. However, it was many years before the true identity of the fossil—a flying reptile—was agreed upon. During the intervening years, many theories evolved to describe the biology of pterosaurs, but most were cast aside in the wake of new discoveries. Until recently, pterosaurs were regarded as an early but inevitably doomed attempt at flight. Cold-blooded and scaly, probably capable of little more than gliding, these animals were seen as a feeble prelude to birds. But these old ideas have now been swept away by new finds.

The first clue came from new studies of the pterosaur's flight apparatus. This is well preserved in remains of *Dimorphodon*. The shape of the sternum and the various bumps

Far right: *Once thought of as unsuccessful gliding prototypes of birds, pterosaurs have been reinstated to their rightful place—commanding the skies of the prehistoric world.*

on the upper arm showed that pterosaurs had large and powerful flight muscles. The shoulder joint was quite complex and, as in birds and bats, enabled the wing to be swept back and forth as well as flapped up and down. The detailed preservation of a 100-million-year-old piece of wing membrane from Brazil also showed that the wing was not just a sheet stretched between the forelimbs and hind limbs, but a complex, layered structure containing muscles that enabled it to control its shape.

The idea of gliding pterosaurs was beginning to seem unlikely, but if they were true fliers, how did they power their wings? Birds and bats have a warm-blooded metabolism capable of sustained flight, but pterosaurs, with a cold-blooded reptilian me-

tabolism, would have been exhausted after only a few minutes. Perhaps pterosaurs had, during the evolution of flight, also become warm-blooded. In the 1960s, a dramatic discovery was made in the Karatau Mountains of Kazakhstan in central Asia. Exquisitely preserved fossils revealed not only details of the wing's shape and extent, but also the presence of numerous fine, short fibers. At last, scientists had found evidence of pterosaur fur and a potentially warm-blooded, high-performance physiology.

Tiny, pitlike openings in the limb bones are further evidence for the warm-blooded theory. As in birds, these openings helped to lighten the skeleton and improve respiration. Once airborne, fliers risk overheating because the activity of the flight muscles gen-

Below: *Even a half-size reconstruction of* Quetzalcoatlus *gives an awe-inspiring impression of how this winged giant must have dominated the air.*

erates so much heat. Pterosaurs evolved a neat solution to this problem. Just under the outer skin the wing membranes contained a layer laced with vessels through which hot blood circulated, dispersing excess heat.

In addition to physiological demands, flight also requires a sophisticated brain. Casts of pterosaur braincases demonstrate that, unlike those of other reptiles, the brain was relatively large, complex, and very bird-like, with well-developed regions concerned with coordination, balance, and vision. Such brains suggest complex behavioral patterns, an idea supported by new interpretations of a common but enigmatic feature of many pterosaurs: skull crests. Crests often rise up from the back of the skull or run along its top surface, and in some recent discoveries large, bladelike crests adorn the tips of the jaws. These distinctive structures were once believed to have had a mechanical function such as steering. But new studies reveal that among particular species they are present on the skulls of some individuals, but not others. This suggests that the crests had a quite different purpose: a display device for intimidating rivals or for attracting mates in courtship rituals.

We now know that pterosaurs, far from being prehistoric flops, were finely tuned to the environment in which they lived. Details of their evolutionary history, including the great length of time for which they existed, show this group to have been very successful. Pterosaurs survived for over 140 million years—at least twice the length of time for which bats have existed and similar to the current age of birds, which first appeared around 150 million years ago.

Pterosaurs also evolved into myriad different forms, as shown by the remarkable variations in how they fed. Many species independently evolved a "fish grab"—a fan of large teeth in the jaw tips that served to pluck fish from the surface of the water. In one case, the lower jaw developed a long,

Above: *The details obtained from fossil finds build a picture complete enough to allow reconstructions such as this one of Pteranodon. A test flight can measure the aerodynamic efficiency of pterosaur physiology.*

prowlike extension, exactly as in the modern black skimmer, that would have plowed the water surface in the hunt for small fish. Other pterosaurs adopted a flamingolike lifestyle, using hundreds of long, fine teeth to filter food from scoops full of water. One group had deep, wide jaws fringed with bristles. These "flying mouths" would have engulfed insect prey in flight, just as swallows and swifts do today. Until recently all pterosaurs were thought to eat flesh, but in the last year a plant-eating form was discovered. With its short, deep, toothless jaws, the skull of this animal looks oddly parrot-like, and it is believed to have fed on fruit and seeds.

Most pterosaurs were only starling- to crow-size, but some became much larger. *Pteranodon,* an oceangoing fish catcher, typically attained wingspans of 10 to 15 feet, although specimens have been found with wingspans up to 30 feet—larger than any bird, living or extinct. These pterosaurs were thought to represent the maximum possible size for a flying animal, until a geologist working in Big Bend National Park in Texas stumbled across the fossil remains of *Quet-*

Right: Pterodaustro *was a filter feeder. It had hundreds of flexible, bristlelike teeth on its lower jaw, through which it could filter tiny aquatic creatures from the water.*

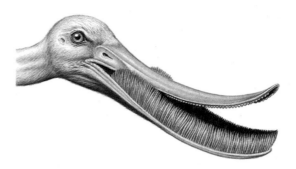

Right: Gallodactylus *had a crest at the back of its skull, which may have been used in a mating display. Sharp teeth confined to the front of the jaws gripped fish.*

Right: Ornithocheirus *had an unusual crest on its upper and lower jaws. These prominent display devices may have been used both to threaten and attract.*

Right: Dsungaripterus *had pointed jaws with toothless tips. It may have used them as pincers to grab heavy scaled fish, cracking them open on bony knobs back in the jaw.*

Right: Dimorphodon *had large front teeth on both jaws with which it snatched up prey. These were followed on each side by 30 to 40 tiny, pointed teeth, which were employed to manipulate the catch.*

zalcoatlus. This animal had a 40-foot wingspan—about the size of a small plane. Other specimens show that this animal had long, toothless jaws and a long neck. It was originally thought that these were adaptations for scavenging the bodies of dead dinosaurs. Another look at the way the neck vertebrae fit together suggests that *Quetzalcoatlus* may have been the ultimate aerial fisher, using its huge wings to soar gently over shallow lakes, then reaching down with its rodlike neck to snap up fish in slender, spear-shaped jaws.

In a joint project with paleontologists, aeronautical engineers tried to recreate the largest flier of all time. Eventually they had to settle for producing a half-size recon-

fossils are the key to understanding the immense history of life, which resulted in the living world that we inhabit today. Great adventures lie ahead, not only for those exploring the cosmos and the heart of the atom, but also for those exploring the extraordinary life of past worlds buried beneath our feet.

David Unwin

Left: *Recent excavations in Brazil yielded a piece of pterosaur wing membrane, miraculously preserved for 100 million years.*

PTEROSAUR ANATOMY

Pterosaurs had birdlike skulls with long, toothed jaws and large eyes. The body was short and compact. The forelimbs carried the wings, the outer halves of which were supported by the elongated fourth finger. This gives us the name ptero-dactyl, *from the Greek* pteros *for "wing" and* dactylos *for "finger." Early forms had long tails with vertical flaps, but these were lost as they evolved.*

How much pterosaurs were able to move on the ground has been fiercely debated. Some argue that pterosaurs tucked their hind limbs up under the body and ran around like birds. But recent studies suggest that the legs sprawled out sideways and were mainly used for controlling the wing membranes. On the ground, pterosaurs probably stood on four limbs and moved slowly and clumsily.

struction, and after a great deal of work, they made a model that flew and even flapped its wings. Unfortunately, it crashed during its first public demonstration but not before more than 20 successful tests, many of which were captured on film.

Pterosaurs and other long extinct groups may appear to have little relevance to the modern world, concerned as it is with problems of global climatic change and threats to biodiversity. Yet the study of such groups forms an integral part of current research programs aimed at understanding past crises in the earth's natural history. In turn, these studies provide insights into the mechanisms that may underlie the current environmental crisis. And beyond the utilitarian,

THE RETURN OF THE WOLF?

Far right: *The gray wolf can be delisted as an endangered species in the northern Rocky Mountains when 10 breeding pairs have been maintained for three years in three areas of native habitat: northwestern Montana, central Idaho, and the Yellowstone area.*

In 1915, the federal government launched a campaign to wipe out the gray wolf, along with all other predators that threatened the interests of western ranchers. By the late 1930s, wolves had virtually disappeared from the West. Today, the government is trying to protect the wolf; in fact, to revitalize its numbers.

There is nothing new about the idea of wolf recovery in the United States. It dates back to 1973, when the Endangered Species Act was passed, mandating protection and restoration of all listed species—including the wolf. What is new is that after 20 years of controversy between wolf advocates and opponents, an end is in sight. In 1994, the Secretary of the Interior is expected to make a decision about the most volatile issue in wolf recovery: the reintroduction of *Canis lupus* into Yellowstone National Park.

Yellowstone is one of three recovery sites designated in the Northern Rocky Mountain Wolf Recovery Plan, which was approved in 1987 by the National Park Service and the U.S. Fish and Wildlife Service. The other sites are northwestern Montana, where approximately 50 wolves have migrated from Canada, and central Idaho, where the number is less than 15. With wolves in residence in both places, natural recolonization is possible if migrants from Canada are encouraged to expand their range. But in Yellowstone, which is highly inaccessible to migrating packs, reintroduction seems to be the only viable route to recovery. That route, however, which calls for importing 10 breeding pairs from Canada, is anathema to many people in the Yellowstone area.

Ranchers are some of the most vociferous opponents of the plan. Wolves will not stay in the park, they say, and that spells economic disaster for nearby sheep and cattle owners. Conservationists reply that with plenty of prey in the park, wolves will not need to travel to find food. Furthermore, even if they do roam, they will not necessarily attack livestock. In Minnesota, the only mainland state with a sizable wolf population (1,500 to 1,750), wolves kill less than one-half of one percent of livestock.

Despite such impressive statistics, pro-wolf groups such as Defenders of Wildlife acknowledge that some livestock depredation is bound to occur. For that reason, the organization has raised $100,000 for a Wolf Compensation Fund with which to reimburse livestock owners for losses. While well intentioned, this solution is far from ideal. Defenders requires proof of a wolf kill, which is frequently difficult to obtain. Moreover, ranchers wonder what will happen when the fund runs out.

Right: *Studies show that bringing the gray wolf to Yellowstone National Park would increase tourist revenues by millions of dollars a year. Polls indicate that most tourists favor the return of the wolf.*

Far right: Since wolves in Yellowstone would be an experimental population, they would be carefully monitored. By equipping the animals with radio collars, researchers can track them and study their habits.

Opposition to the reintroduction plan also comes from local hunting industries and commodity producers. Both groups fear that wolf management on public lands will result in restrictions on hunting, mining, logging, and drilling. Hunting outfitters also contend that wolves will deplete big game, causing severe losses in hunting revenues. Conservationists believe these concerns are exaggerated. They point out that wolves are highly adaptable, so special habitat considerations would be minimal. Moreover, there is plenty of prey for both man and beast, especially since hunters tend to take healthy prime-age animals, while wolves usually prey on the old, young, and sick.

Such reassurances have done little to sway the antiwolf camp. In the face of such strong opposition, a question arises: why Yellowstone? Why not choose a less controversial reintroduction site?

That the park is prime habitat for the gray wolf is only one part of the answer. Of equal, some say even greater, importance is the fact that Yellowstone needs the wolf. In its absence, the animal's prey populations have become dangerously inflated. As a result, overgrazing by elk, deer, moose, and bighorn sheep has caused shortages of food. Thus, the wolf is needed to restore the balance in the park's ecosystem.

In addition, the Park Service has a mandate to maintain and restore all of the native flora and fauna in our national parks. "Gray wolves are the only animals missing from Yellowstone," says the park's chief biologist, John Varley. "If we restore them, it would be the only place in the lower 48 states that would have all the fauna that were here when Christopher Columbus stepped ashore."

So strongly do conservationists feel about returning the wolf to Yellowstone that many are willing to compromise in order to attain

Right: Wolves generally hunt animals that are larger than themselves, like the elk shown here. An adult wolf may eat 5 to 12 pounds of meat per day, depending on the availability of food.

that goal. Most major prowolf groups have endorsed a proposal to designate reintroduced wolves a "nonessential experimental" population. Under this classification the animals would lose some of the protection they now enjoy as an endangered species, while local agencies would gain more options for controlling wolves outside of protected areas.

The "experimental" classification is one of a number of proposals that are being considered in an Environmental Impact Statement (EIS), which the U.S. Fish and Wildlife Service is currently preparing. The purpose of the EIS is to examine all the issues involved in returning the gray wolf to Yellowstone and to elicit public opinion on the subject. A draft EIS, covering a variety of alternatives about reintroduction, is due out in May 1993. The final document will be released in 1994—the year of the wolf, if conservationists have their way.

Alice Quine

WOLVES & THEIR WAYS

Wolves are intelligent, highly social creatures that live in packs, which usually consist of eight to ten related members. Each pack is dominated by an alpha male and female that mate for life. Breeding is generally restricted to the alpha couple, and the pack may include several generations of their offspring.

Depending on the availability of food, a pack holds a territory of 70 to 800 square miles. The members will tolerate no intruders. If scent and howls fail to deter an outsider, a pack will attack it.

Howling not only serves as a warning to intruders, it also keeps the pack together. Wolves communicate using other sounds as well, including aggressive growls and submissive or friendly whimpers. Such vocalizations plus various postures help to maintain the pack's social structure.

Pack members begin to form strong bonds at an early age. The entire group participates in rearing the young, protecting and playing with them. Pups elicit meals from an adult by nuzzling its mouth—a signal that prompts the wolf to regurgitate food. The youngsters

also form strong attachments to their littermates, engaging in playful fights and even sharing their food.

Such bonds are necessary for the survival of the pack, which depends on cooperation. The animals hunt communally, relying on teamwork to bring down big game. Because they often wound prey before moving in for the kill, wolves have been labeled vicious killers. Yet they are merely following the laws of nature that govern the relationship between predators and their prey. Ironically, wolves have been most maligned as mankillers—a reputation they least deserve. In North America, there are no documented records of a healthy (nonrabid) wolf trying to kill a human being.

LIVING THE HIGH LIFE

Right: *Only recently have ingenious contraptions such as the "sky raft" enabled naturalists to remain in the rainforest canopy for long periods, observing the life of its myriad inhabitants.*

Below: *The red-eyed tree frog finds a vital water source in the base of the leaves of a huge bromeliad plant.*

One of the last scientific frontiers lies not light years away in space or deep beneath the world's oceans but about 150 feet above the ground. This is where the trees of lowland rainforest spread their branches to reach the sun, forming a vast green roof, or canopy.

Until 10 years ago, the canopy was quite literally out of reach. Biologists who tried to climb up the vast, smooth tree trunks were met by armies of stinging, biting insects, poisonous snakes, and other animals. Then, using newly developed lightweight materials, scientists began to build ladders and towers to get to the branches, slinging rope bridges and trapezes from one tree across to the next. Some scientists even descended on the rainforest canopy from above, suspended in gondolas held by massive industrial cranes.

What is emerging from these explorations is the importance of this unique environment: it is now thought to contain more than half of all life, and a single rainforest tree may harbor more than 10,000 species. In the 1970s, American biologists believed that there were approximately 10 million insect species in the world; estimates now stand at about 50 million. Yet even as these species are being discovered, their existence is being threatened. Humans have destroyed half the world's tropical rainforests in the last 50 years, and, according to the World Wide Fund for Nature, an area the size of Minnesota is still being cleared every year. Nine-tenths of Central America's rainforests have already been cleared, while in Madagascar and Paraguay the rainforests will be gone in 20 years unless the rate of tree cutting is controlled.

"Rainforest" is a fairly broad term used to describe many different kinds of forest. The popular image of tall evergreen trees and dense humidity applies to lowland tropical rainforest. Montane rainforest, sometimes called cloud forest, has a lower canopy and is cooler and drier. Coastal mangrove forest is also a type of rainforest. Farther from the equator, in areas of lower rainfall, grows semideciduous tropical forest.

Seen from the air, lowland rainforest appears as a solid mass of leaves, but actually it is made up of many layers that blend into one another. Uppermost is the dry, hot, sunny realm of the treetops, their crowns spreading out but not quite touching one another. Their average height is about 150 feet, but giant emergent trees grow to heights of 200 feet or more. Beneath the canopy roof, branches are festooned with climbing plants and epiphytes. Under them is another story—a network of smaller trees, fighting for sunlight in the humid gloom of the inner forest.

Each habitat offers a microenvironment to suit different species. Sunshine and food are available all year round in equatorial forests, so neither plants nor animals need to be as adaptable to change as those in temperate lands. In fact, specialization is the best option. Over millions of years, rainfor-

competition with its relatives by exploiting the various food sources that are found among the lower branches, between the two extremes.

The earth-shattering roar of the howler monkey is no idle display. Different troops of these social monkeys rove through the canopy, calling to warn of their current position. In this way they can exploit the forest's foliage and fruit while avoiding skirmishes between competing troops.

Canopy-dwelling animals have evolved remarkable physical adaptations for their high-rise life, and for those at the very top, flight is the best method of movement. We generally think of flying insects, birds, and bats, but there are also "flying" squirrels, frogs, lizards, and even snakes. None of these can really fly, but they have adaptations for leaping or gliding between trees. The golden flying snake has specialized ribs that allow it to flatten its body and "swim" through the air for up to 10 feet. The flying dragon has wings supported by rib extensions and can glide for distances of 55 feet.

The colugos of Southeast Asia are the best aviators of all and can glide for up to 330 feet. They have a membrane that encompasses all four limbs—stretching from the chin to the tip of the tail—which gives

Above: *This plant, a philodendron, attaches its aerial roots to a tree. Trees are the best routes to light in the dim forest, and by growing up the trunk of the tree, the plant reaches the sun.*

Right: *Birds such as the green-winged macaw forage for fruit and berries in the forest.*

est dwellers have adapted to their particular environmental niche, so that many have formed relationships with other, often totally dissimilar, species.

The challenges of life in different layers of the canopy are met in a variety of ways by different species. To avoid conflict over territory or food sources, for example, they may stay in a particular story or stake their claim to an area by calling loudly. Among the opossums of South America, which all feed on invertebrates, the woolly opossums live high in the trees, while gray and southern opossums keep mainly to the forest floor. The common mouse opossum avoids

these cat-size mammals the appearance of an animated kite.

Flying is difficult in the lower canopy; birds, bats, and insects all use regular flight paths to avoid branches. Some spiders spin their webs across these well-used routes to catch flies and butterflies.

For larger animals, leaping and climbing are better options. Leaping animals are typically light, small, and agile. Lemurs and monkeys have grasping hands, and the monkeys of South and Central America have the additional advantage of prehensile tails. The sakis of Colombia can cross distances of up to 100 feet in a single leap.

Heavy mammals such as orangutans tend to stay among the lower, stronger branches. The orangutan does not leap across gaps, but instead sways its tree until it comes within grabbing range of the next branch, at which point it transfers its weight and allows the first tree to spring back. The tarsier leaps like a tree frog between creepers and tree trunks, kicking off with its powerful hind legs.

The slow loris, a small relative of the bush baby, has developed the latter's particular method of movement for stealth rather than speed. As its name suggests, the slow loris moves incredibly slowly and carefully, as if in a slow-motion film, to catch resting insects and birds off guard. The blood vessels in its limbs are exceptionally good, and the slow loris can remain motionless for hours without developing muscle cramp.

The three-toed sloth's leafy diet is low in nutrients, so it moves as little as possible in order to conserve energy. Its locking claws enable it to hang effortlessly from branches, where its coat of algae-encrusted hairs hides it from predators.

Plants, too, have adapted to life in the rainforest canopy. The most important of these are epiphytes, sometimes known as air plants. Their seeds settle in nooks on branches and trunks high above the ground, wherever there are a few grains of leaf mold or dust to support them. It is thought that there are about 28,000 species of epiphyte worldwide, including many mosses, liverworts, ferns, lichens, orchids, bromeliads, and even some cacti.

Epiphytes take all of their food from the sun and the rain, as well as the debris that settles around them. Decaying leaves, animal droppings, and dead insects all accumulate and are tapped for food, and many epiphytes even have water reservoirs in the base of their leaves. Gradually, an epiphyte mat builds up on the topsides of tree limbs. Branches used as highways by forest animals can be distinguished because constant trampling keeps them clear of all but the smallest plants.

There are advantages and disadvantages

Left: *The flower mantis uses its resemblance to a plant to attract insect prey—then it strikes out for the kill.*

Below: *The three-toed sloth is in no hurry for its leafy meal. It expends as little energy as it can in its movements.*

Above: *Researchers on long-term observation projects are rushing to gain knowledge before forests are cut down for lumber and entire species are lost.*

for host and guest alike. The tree loses some sunlight and gains the weight of the epiphytes, but many trees have evolved aerial roots that can take food and water from the nutrient-rich mat. For the guest plants there is the benefit of a shortcut to the sun, but this is set against the risk of death if the overloaded branch breaks or the tree falls.

Bromeliads are epiphytes whose strap-like leaves resemble those of a giant pineapple; in fact, they are members of the same plant family. Both are also minute habitats, with water reservoirs that are useful for many animals in the hot canopy. These tiny ponds attract tree frogs, salamanders, and spiders, as well as the many kinds of insects that lay their eggs in the water of the ready-made nurseries.

Other arboreal plants literally keep one foot on the ground. Lianas root in the ground but take hold on nearby trees on a light-seeking climb to the canopy, extending tendrils for support. Strangling figs work the opposite way—their seeds are scattered through the canopy in the droppings of birds and monkeys. When a seed germinates, it sends a root down to the ground. The fig then puts out leaves and more roots, which eventually throttle the host tree.

Some trees escape from the clutches of climbers. The *Cecropia* employs Azteca ants as guardians. The ants live in the tree's hollow branches and feed on nectar from its leaves, protecting the tree by cutting away young epiphytes and creeper tendrils. Epiphytes receive a warmer welcome from other ant species: one Asian species has a symbiotic relationship with its ant tenants, which shelter in its hollow root chambers. The plant secretes nectar, which the ants eat, in turn defending their host from animals and other plants.

Despite their name, leaf-cutter ants, found only in the Americas, do not eat leaves. Individuals cut pieces of leaves from plants and trees and take them back to the nest. There, they chew them to a pulp into which they sow fungus spores. The leaf pulp provides a compost bed for the growing fungus, which the ants harvest and eat.

In many habitats the wind is an important carrier of pollen and seeds, but it barely penetrates the dense rainforest. Instead, plants bribe flying insects, birds, and bats with nectar and fruit to get their flowers pollinated and their seeds spread over a wide area. Flowers often fit one particular species of insect, increasing the chance of it carrying pollen from one bloom to another. Not all insects eat nectar; many are predators. One such, the flower mantis, looks just like a flower itself and uses its disguise to catch other insects as they land on its "petals."

Reaching the Top

Getting into the rainforest canopy has been the goal of naturalists for generations, but until recently it was less attainable than Mount Everest. The first serious attempts to reach it were made in the 1920s by a team from Oxford University on an expedition to Guyana. The team met with very limited success.

Different approaches during the 1960s and '70s involved the use of platforms, towers, and bridges but all were too cumbersome to be of much use.

In 1978, Stephen Sutton, a tropical ecologist, and Andrew Mitchell (above right), a zoologist, designed a lightweight aerial walkway. In Panama, Andrew reached the canopy 100 feet above the ground.

Since 1987 in French Guiana, Francis Hallé and his colleagues have been making use of a remarkable "sky raft," measuring 6,460 square feet in area. Using ropes and harnesses, scientists can climb up to it from the forest floor below.

Adaptation and interdependence allow survival in the stable environment of the rainforest, but the whole arrangement is extremely fragile. If one species is wiped out, its dependents die too. There are, for example, at least 80 species of fig in Amazonia, each pollinated by its own species of wasp. Localized populations are vulnerable to extinction, and even limited tree cutting may destroy the delicate balance.

For the energetic breed of biologists now exploring the canopies of rainforests, it is a race against time to find and record even a fraction of what lives there, to understand just a little more of the world to which we belong, before any more decks of this wonderful house of cards collapse.

Sarah Foster

Left: *Dr. Jellison, an Australian researcher, uses special optical equipment that makes it easier to examine small specimens.*

Overleaf: *The orangutan is less nimble than many canopy inhabitants. It stays among the lower branches, which are sturdy enough to bear its weight.*

69

ENVIRONMENTAL ISSUES

When people think of the environment, they usually focus on the world's endangered animals and habitats. While these are undeniably vital issues in the struggle to save the planet, the most challenging question may be how humans can fit into an environmentally secure world.

With this consideration in mind, we open this section with a report on the results of the Earth Summit in Rio de Janeiro. We next look at the way humans deplete the oceans' resources when fishing for food and then examine another crisis caused largely by human activity—the critically poor health of western forests in the United States.

We also survey the world's forgotten conservationists— the indigenous people who have plenty to teach us about living in harmony with our environment. Closer to home is an introduction to converting your own backyard into a wildlife habitat. Then, after an exploration of wildlife-friendly tourism, we end in the remote Galápagos Islands, where tourism is managed in the best interests of the region's unique wildlife.

Left: *Global changes in climate may heighten the effects of desertification in areas such as Mali in West Africa, making life impossible to sustain.*

Below left: *Indigenous people such as the Inuit possess traditional lifestyles that enable them to live from the land without depleting natural resources.*

Below: *Rainforests not only serve as convenient "clearing stations" for the greenhouse gases emitted by the developed world. They are also an essential habitat for the humans and wildlife that live in them.*

THE ROAD FROM RIO

The Rio Conference may turn out to be a turning point in human history and in our relationship with the 30 million or so other species with which we share the planet. Or it could be a brief interruption on the road to the destruction of the earth's wild areas and, ultimately, ourselves.

The Earth Summit, held by the United Nations (UN) in Rio de Janeiro in June 1992, was the largest-ever gathering of heads of state and other government representatives, who met to discuss the economic development and environmental protection of the planet. The Summit's organizers hoped that world leaders would respond to the central message that protecting nature is essential to economic progress.

The Summit's program covered almost every aspect of human activity. Its fundamental themes included biodiversity, climate change, forests, desertification, and sustainable development.

The planet is losing plant and animal species and the lands they inhabit at an unprecedented rate. At the Summit more than 150 nations signed the Biodiversity Convention, aimed at finding ways to protect species and habitats. Its particular goals are to protect forests from clearance, forestall drainage of wetlands, and stop the plowing and fencing of grasslands.

Air pollution from burning coal and oil threatens to alter global climates through the so-called greenhouse effect. By melting ice caps, causing rises in sea level, it could also drown low-lying areas and islands. These processes would endanger wildlife and humans. In Rio, more than 150 countries signed the Climate Convention, agree-

Above: *It remains to be seen whether the world's nations can take political action and fulfill the ideals of the Rio Conference.*

Right: *Nestling at dusk between the hills and the sea, Rio glows with beauty, but on the crowded streets poverty is rarely out of sight.*

Right: *Where forests have been cleared for wheat and other crops in western Australia, the land is prone to erosion. It is estimated that, for every pound of bread Australia produces, seven pounds of topsoil are lost.*

Far right: *Despite their massive populations, developing countries use only a fraction of the energy consumed by the industrialized nations.*

Right: *The Amazon Pilot Project, proposed at the Summit, will help conserve habitat for the rare bearded saki.*

ing to the development of national strategies preventing further increases in emissions of greenhouse gases.

All nations agreed on a Statement of Forest Principles. This is a weaker document than the Forest Convention, which some countries had wanted, but it still commits nations to trying to save their forests. This applies as much to the United States, with its relatively few surviving ancient woodlands, as to countries with vast rainforests.

The world's deserts are growing due to a mixture of drought and overuse of fragile soils in dry lands. In these arid areas, such as the Sahel region on the edge of the Sahara Desert, live some of the world's poorest people, who depend on the poor soil to grow food or graze livestock. The Summit agreed that a Desertification Convention should be drawn up in the next two years for a worldwide fight against this menace.

Western governments made commitments to ensure that their loans to Third World countries would take more notice of the environmental impact of projects such as large dams and power stations, irrigation programs, or forestry. Environmentally damaging projects are frequently not economically sustainable. Foresters may run out of trees to cut, or irrigation channels may become clogged with weeds.

Despite these initiatives, by many yardsticks the Summit was a failure. Maurice Strong, the Canadian oil millionaire turned environmental impresario who organized the Summit, said beforehand that an extra $10 billion in "green aid" to the Third World was necessary to set the world on a path to "sustainable development." The entire package of measures discussed in Rio might cost $600 billion a year to implement, with a fifth of that coming in aid. But by the end of the Summit, Strong estimated that only an extra $6 billion a year had been raised, and less than $2 billion of that was certain.

Besides lack of money, there were serious problems with the global policing of rainforests that had been intended by the Statement of Forest Principles. Roughly half the world's plant and animal species may live in rainforests. But Third World nations, notably Malaysia and India, were angered by President Bush's statement before the Summit that he wanted to preserve forests partly to soak up some of the gases emitted by cars and power stations in the wealthy nations. One Malaysian delegate told British journalists: "If you want international control of our forests, then we think there should be international control of North Sea oil, the source of much of your pollution."

Oil figured in other thoughts, too. The great clouds of black smoke from burning Kuwaiti oil fields and the slicks that suffocated fish and killed coral in the Persian Gulf were grim reminders of how the environment could be used as a weapon of war. Strong opened the Earth Summit by saying: "War . . . is a major source of environmental damage, which must be subject to greater accountability and control. This should include much stronger legal instruments . . . [to] provide effective deterrence against future environmental aggressors."

But many nations, including the United States, opposed this idea, and it disappeared without a trace from the final agreements.

There were other gaps. The Third World did not want to talk about overpopulation, which is forcing humans to take over wild lands. Rich countries would not discuss overconsumption and how they might use less of the world's resources. But despite the failures, there were some signs of how the world could improve after Rio.

One of the biggest beneficiaries from the Summit was the host, Brazil. It will get most of the $150 million President Bush committed before the Summit opened as the initial phase in doubling U.S. aid for the earth's forests. At the top of the list is the Amazon Pilot Project, which will cost rich nations $250 million in the next three years.

This project will contribute to protecting the Amazon rainforest in several ways. It will pay for policing national parks and large new reserves for indigenous communities. It will help establish "extractive reserves" for rubber tappers in the remote state of Acre. Here the tappers will be able to maintain the forests and harvest rubber from trees, without their land being taken over by speculators, lumber companies, or itinerant peasants from the east. These policies will help preserve animals such as the giant otter, one of the world's rarest otters, and the southern bearded saki, the most endangered primate in Amazonia.

The Amazon project will also pay for research into new uses for rainforest plants —from fruit flavors for Western ice creams and cosmetics for the Body Shop, to extracting chemicals from plants to treat diseases such as cancer and AIDS.

Similar work around the world will also be greatly encouraged by the Biodiversity Convention, signed by most nations in Rio. This commits countries to promoting deals where Western money pays Third World countries to make better use of their forests and other wild areas. In return, Third World countries promise foreign companies better access to their great biological wealth. There was consternation in Rio because the United States refused to sign the Biodiversity Convention. All the major European nations signed. Maurice Strong said he believed that the United States would eventually "find a way to sign."

President Bush objected that some of the Convention's provisions threatened U.S. jobs. He was concerned about patent rights to new products from forests and safety rules on new products involving biotechnology. But the head of the UN Environment Program, Mostafa Tolba, warned that the U.S. companies would be frozen out of deals with Third World nations to exploit their forests if the government did not sign.

The potential importance of such deals is summed up by the case of the rosy periwinkle from Madagascar. A chemical from this plant has provided a cure for Hodgkin's disease worth more than $100 million in sales each year. A study for the World Wide Fund for Nature stated that "if Madagascar had received a significant part of this income, it would have been one of the country's largest sources of income." As it is, the country gained nothing. Under the

Biodiversity Convention, future finds could give poor tropical nations large incomes. This should encourage them to preserve their forests and to let foreign companies enter them. In such ways, it is hoped that environmental protection and economic growth can go hand in hand.

However, much depends on the world's climates. There is no proof, but the man-made greenhouse effect is being blamed for everything from droughts in Africa and the Far East, to the sudden arrival of tropical cyclones in previously tranquil South Pacific islands. In Indonesia, drought caused massive forest fires to rage through late 1991 and much of 1992, especially in Sumatra, the home of the fewer than 500 surviving Sumatran rhinos. In Western Samoa in the Pacific, much of the forest was recently battered by Hurricane Val. Deaths among the local population of flying foxes, which disperse seeds, may prevent the forests from recovering. In Africa, the drought that has lasted for two decades may wipe out many of the continent's surviving grasslands.

These are just the first signs of potentially cataclysmic changes in climate around the globe—changes that, biologists say, could

Above: *All peoples were represented at the Summit, with each delegate bringing a unique set of needs.*

Far left: *The clearcutting of ancient forests in Washington State points to the problem of habitat destruction even in wealthy countries.*

Left: *Rainforest plants may have endless medical applications. The beguilingly named hot-lips plant of Belize is used locally as a natural contraceptive.*

wipe out many of the most productive wild lands of the planet. Nowhere is safe, from the immense conifer forests of Siberia and northern Canada, which extend almost as far as the tropical rainforests, to the precious wetlands of Brazil's Pantanal, home of the capybara, jaguar, and spectacled caiman. For wetlands, changes in rainfall could be as damaging as global warming.

Studies commissioned by the United Nations for the Earth Summit confirmed that a 60 percent cut worldwide in emissions of greenhouse gases is needed to stabilize climates. If not, as Strong said at the start of the Summit, "the changes in the next 60 years may be so rapid that nature will be unable to adapt and man incapable of controlling them."

Yet the target in the Climate Convention to stabilize emissions at 1990 levels by the year 2000 is just that—a target, not a commitment. At the close of the Summit, Strong called the greenhouse effect "the most urgent crisis we face" and the failure to tackle it the Summit's most serious failure.

Some Third World nations claimed that worrying about a future climate crisis was a luxury they could not afford. Their people

Below: *Coral reefs embody a pressing environmental problem: what takes centuries to develop can be wiped out in days by human thoughtlessness.*

had to be fed first, whatever the ecological cost. But for others it was a matter of national survival: recent studies show that the rise in sea levels as ice caps melt in a warmed world will drown them.

"For some islands it may be too late," said Robert van Lieerp, ambassador for Vanuatu, which—with Tuvalu, Kiribati, and the Marshall Islands—is among the most threatened of the tiny coral islands in the Pacific.

The loss of such islands would be a biological as well as a human tragedy. Rising waters already threaten to outpace the growth of coral reefs and thus destroy them. Coral reefs are the marine equivalent of the tropical rainforests. They harbor a huge diversity of species. And, like forests, they have a great ability to absorb carbon from the air and surface waters, counteracting the greenhouse effect. In addition to life on the coral reefs, there are a large number of unique plant and animal species on land, in the surviving forests of the Pacific islands.

The Earth Summit is only the start of a process that environmentalists hope will bring some ecological sanity back to the world. "This could be our last, best chance," Strong said. During 1993, we should see flesh put on the bones of Rio. The Climate and Biodiversity Conventions could be in place, with the first national plans published by Western countries to show how they will limit their emissions of greenhouse gases. Negotiations should get under way for the Desertification Treaty and perhaps for the long-delayed Forest Convention. World production of the CFCs that destroy the ozone layer should continue to drop quickly, in line with agreements made before Rio. Most important, perhaps, there should be the first meetings of the UN Commission for Sustainable Development, which is intended as the first permanent watchdog of the planet's environment.

But all that is just bureaucracy. The world still awaits the first year when more trees

Left: *Recent research suggests that mangrove forests, which sustain important tropical fisheries, would not survive the fast rises in sea level that may result from global warming.*

are planted than are cut or burned down; the first year when fewer greenhouse gases are put into the atmosphere than the year before; a reduction in the number of people drinking disease-ridden water and going to bed starving; and a time when animal species are taken off the endangered list not because they are extinct but because they are flourishing.

If the Earth Summit succeeds in its aims, then all these "firsts" could soon be hitting the headlines.

Fred Pearce

Below: *Intent mainly on sustaining their exports, governments are doing little to control the proliferation of cars, which are inflicting untold damage on the environment.*

FISHING FOR FOOD

Right: *As world trade expands, more and more fish are caught to be sold on the international market.*

Far right: *Spotter planes and echo sounders are now widely used to locate schools of fish.*

Below: *The most recent figures (1989) show world fish catches of about 100 million tons—a record high.*

More than 70 percent of the planet is covered with water, at an average depth of two and a half miles—making the seas the largest habitat for life on earth. Fish live in all waters, from the poles to the tropics, and have been caught for food since time immemorial. Until very recently, the sea and the food it offered were treated as an infinite resource. Today, this illusion is no longer sustainable, and we are facing the consequences of our heedless exploitation of this precious environment.

Not only do fish provide humans with a valuable source of protein, but at least 40 percent of the world catch is used to make fish meal to feed livestock or to utilize as a fertilizer. This is a highly inefficient use, since by the time the fish is processed, much of its protein content is lost.

For most of human history, the main kind of fishing was "artisanal fishing"—small-scale fishing on coastal and inshore waters, as well as rivers and lakes. Although today artisanal fishing accounts for only a tenth of the world's fish catch, in many developing countries it still supplies 40 to 100 percent of the animal protein in people's diets.

The range of techniques used for artisanal fishing is remarkable. Many methods are designed to trap fish moving offshore when the tide ebbs. Since prehistoric times, Fijians have used a simple semicircular wall of rocks that becomes exposed at low tide, stranding the fish. In other places, in estuaries and narrow inlets, gill nets are strung across the water. The fish cannot see these nets of fine twine and become trapped by their gill covers. Nets of different mesh sizes are used to catch various sizes of fish.

Where water currents run parallel to the shore, nets or fences are set to funnel fish into narrow-mouthed enclosures that are fixed to the seabed or suspended between small boats—a process sometimes aided by shouting and splashing fishermen. An even simpler device is a bundle of brushwood placed in the water to catch fish living on the bottom. These fish tend to seek shelter, so they congregate in the brushwood. Lobsters have the same habit, and all over the world they are trapped in thorn-lined traps or baskets with a small narrow entrance, often baited with rotting fish or shellfish.

A fishing method known to all small children is the rod and baited line, a technique that can be used even in quite deep water. A more active kind of artisanal fishing is to walk through muddy shallow water and trap fish under hand-held pots as the feet disturb them.

In clear water, sharp-eyed fishermen use spears to hunt octopus and other shallow-water species. Even more skill is needed to use a cast net—a circular net some 30 feet across that is thrown by hand so that it opens just as it hits the water. Weights on its edge pull the net down, trapping schools of fish as it sinks to the bottom.

Small fishing communities adjust their activities to the seasonal migrations of the fish. They often supplement fishing with activities such as farming during the rest of

Above: *Traditional fishing techniques allow stocks to recover just enough to supply local communities. Whether the fish supply will be able to survive modern economic pressures is now seriously in doubt.*

the year. Each generation hands down its knowledge about the seasonal movements of fish, where they spawn and where they feed, helping to prevent overfishing.

Although these simple practices may not seem to pose any threat to stocks, many small fishing communities are near tourist developments, which provide new local markets. In addition, the resorts have road, rail, and air links that bring more distant markets within reach. Selling fish for cash then becomes a viable option.

Many artisanal fisheries are increasingly threatened, however. Inshore, growing settlements and expanding tourism pose a range of problems, including pollution, the blasting of reefs for building materials, and the cutting of mangrove forests for fuel and construction materials. Coral reefs in particular are vulnerable to pollution, since corals can survive only in clear water. In addition, soil washes down from eroding inland areas and silts up many coastal reefs.

Another problem is the growth of commercial fleets, which operate just outside national waters used by local populations. The technology now exists to catch fish in quantities beyond the dreams of artisanal fishermen. Modern fishing vessels fall into three main categories. Factory trawlers drag weighted nets along the continental shelves to catch bottom-dwelling fish such as cod, hake, and haddock, which are then transported on ice back to port.

For fish living closer to the surface, giant purse seiners are used. Their huge nets can encircle entire shoals, and the ships can carry over 150 tons of frozen fish. Modern nets can sweep up a whole shoal in a single pass, and as stocks become smaller and more scattered, ever more sophisticated boats are built to find them. This technique is used for far-ranging fish such as bluefin tuna, marlin, and sailfish.

Yellowfin tuna, which swim deeper, are trapped with longlines—strings of baited hooks extending over 18 miles from the ship. Marlin and sailfish are also trapped on longlines. Technology is now so advanced that the Japanese are developing robots to carry out this labor-intensive form of fishing.

A tragic consequence of commercial fishing is that throughout the oceans of the world millions of dolphins, turtles, and other marine animals die every year, entangled in huge nylon drift nets—some over 30 miles long—which are strung out across the sea. Many of these nets break away from their vessels and drift across the oceans, becoming vast "walls of death" that continue to "fish" for decades.

Another result of the increased efficiency of the fishing industry is that many stocks have been seriously overfished. This has led to a decline in the number of whales, fur seals, and sea otters. There has also been a drop in anchovy stocks off the Peruvian coast, declining catches off the Newfoundland Grand Banks, dwindling salmon runs in various rivers, and diminishing cod and herring stocks in the North Sea.

Another, less expected consequence of intensive fishing has been the decrease in average size of the fish caught. Since it is mainly the larger, more mature fish that are caught, individuals that breed at an early age, at a smaller body size, are more likely to produce offspring. Over time, this forced genetic selection produces smaller species. During the late 19th century, Atlantic cod weighed as much as 200 pounds; today the largest weigh about 24 pounds.

Overfishing of one species can affect others, and today there is cause for concern about the fishing of Antarctic krill. These shrimplike creatures are central to the food chain of the southern oceans—providing the staple diet of the great whales and crabeater seals, as well as countless seabirds. We do not know what impact the loss of vast

Above: *The breeding success of puffins in the Shetland Islands, near Scotland, has recently dropped—probably because of overfishing of the sand eels that they feed their young.*

Left: *Deep-sea trawlers are not selective in the fish species they catch. They can cause untold damage to the seabed and its wildlife.*

Right: *Aquaculture has been carried out in the Far East for thousands of years. But today, with growing populations, more and more coastal habitats are being cleared with little thought for wildlife.*

Below: *Deep-water fish often grow slowly. The orange roughie, for example, cannot breed until it is 20 years old. Off New Zealand's coast, a fishing industry barely 12 years old has already reduced local orange roughie stocks by 60 to 70 percent.*

numbers of krill will have on other animals.

Unfortunately, only declining catches persuade national governments to introduce limits on fishing operations, but these measures are often too little, too late. The setting of quotas has been a popular but highly questionable way of limiting catches. Fishermen who want to extract the most revenue from their quota throw back undersized or unwanted fish. Limiting the number of days of fishing or the number of boats only leads to the development of better methods of locating and catching fish, so that more are caught on each trip.

It is estimated that up to 90 percent of the world's fish stocks are already exploited at the maximum sustainable level. With the decline in these stocks, new sources are continually being investigated.

The farming of fish—aquaculture—is now a growth industry. It consists of keeping fish and shellfish in pens and boosting their food supply artificially. Commercial aquaculture accounts for almost one-fifth of the total world fisheries production today.

Milkfish are the main cultivated fish in Southeast Asia, where rearing fish boosts the income and food supply of small-scale farmers. Increasingly, tilapia, silver barb, and common carp—all plant-eating fish—are reared in paddy fields. Farm wastes can help boost the growth of algae, and the addition of pelleted food enhances the fish's diet. Tilapia are farmed in other tropical areas, while trout and carp are farmed in cooler regions. Salmon are the main saltwater fish farmed in temperate regions.

With the growth of fish farming, however, natural habitats inevitably suffer. One-third of Ecuador's mangrove forests were destroyed for prawn production between 1979 and 1983. The Philippines has lost some 60 percent of its mangroves to aquaculture since the 1920s. Yet the habitats being destroyed are vital nurseries for the fish

ments. Until recently, self-regulation by countries or groups of countries, such as the European Community, or by special organizations, such as the Inter-American Tropical Tuna Commission, was the rule. But this system has been breaking down. With the decline of fish stocks that range across national boundaries, international disputes over fishing rights are more common.

Since the 1960s a convention on the Law of the Sea has been negotiated, giving individual countries the right to set up Exclusive Economic Zones (EEZs) extending up to 206 miles offshore. But the new Law of the Sea has not yet been ratified by enough countries to have much impact.

An important recent achievement was the 1989 UN resolution that banned all high-seas drift netting from mid-1992. Increasing international pressure for conservation of fish stocks may eventually modify the centuries-old treatment of fish as the common property of anyone capable of harvesting them.

Jill Bailey

on which many artisanal fisheries depend. Moreover, shrimp and prawn cultivation is often based on a supply of wild juveniles, which ultimately depletes wild stocks.

Intensive farming of fish and shellfish results in certain typical problems, such as the rapid spread of disease and parasites, which may escape and attack wild populations. Chemicals added to control disease enter the surrounding waters, where they kill marine life. Waste food and fish excreta travel to the nearby sea, resulting in algal blooms. An additional concern is that escaped fish may upset the delicate genetic balance of wild fish.

Many of these local problems are gradually being tackled by national legislation. The worldwide decline of fish stocks has a much greater economic impact, and it is now being combated by international agree-

Left: *In the shallow waters of Marlborough Sands in New Zealand, mussels are dredged from natural beds to be farmed. Young larvae settle naturally on the bottom, and the tides supply them with fresh food twice daily.*

FUEL FOR FIRE

Right: *Wildfires are more helpful than harmful to forest animals. Fire lets grasses and other foods grow by thinning thick stands of trees so light can penetrate to the forest floor.*

Far right: *One of 1992's worst wildfires was in California's Shasta-Trinity National Forest, where 7,500 people had to be evacuated.*

Below: *Fire is essential in the lifecycle of certain trees. Sequoias, for example, need extreme heat to release the seeds from their cones.*

The summer of 1992 marked the sixth season of drought in the West, with forest fires that burned some one million acres. In Northern California alone, six major wildfires broke out in less than a week during the middle of August. The most devastating was the Fountain Fire, which consumed 64,000 acres in the Shasta-Trinity National Forest before firefighters managed to control it.

While a period of drought always puts a forest under stress, it does not explain the increased number and severity of wildfires in recent years. That explanation lies in the critically poor health of many western forests, where insect damage has reached epidemic proportions. The problem is most severe east of the Cascades in the Pacific Northwest, with millions of acres of trees damaged or killed by spruce budworms, tussock moths, and bark beetles.

Many experts agree that more than a century of selective logging has weakened the forests, leaving them vulnerable to insects and disease. Oregon's Blue Mountains, for example, were stripped of the economically valuable, insect-resistant ponderosa pine and larch that once dominated the forests. In their absence, less-resistant species proliferated; in particular, fir, spruce, and lodgepole pine.

Ironically, decades of fire suppression contributed to the problem in our western forests. The Forest Service's policy of extinguishing all fires made no exception for the frequent small blazes that are nature's way of thinning forests. The result was severe overcrowding, with too many trees competing for moisture and nutrients. Such conditions produce weak trees, unable to resist insects and disease. Ultimately, decay sets in, deadwood builds up, and the entire forest becomes fuel for all-consuming fire.

The fire-suppression policy came into question in the 1960s when scientists began studying the role of natural fire in forest ecology. They found that periodic, low-intensity blazes tend to prevent uncontrollable conflagrations by keeping deadwood and brush from accumulating on the forest floor. In addition, small fires pave the way for healthy new growth—a fact that Native Americans discovered centuries ago. Indians often set fires, knowing that once new growth appeared, game would follow.

In light of these findings, the Forest Service launched a new fire-management policy in 1972. Under specific prescribed conditions, natural wildfires were allowed to burn in order to reduce fuel buildup in many national forests. For the same purpose and under the same guidelines, prescribed fires could also be ignited. These guidelines permitted burning only in areas where human lives and economic interests would not be threatened and only when weather conditions were favorable. In all cases, "prescribed burns" were strictly supervised by trained fire managers.

Right: *When wildfires break out in inaccessible regions, they are often fought by Forest Service Smokejumpers, who parachute into the area.*

By 1988 controlled burning had become an established part of fire-management policy in wilderness areas. But during the summer of that year, the policy came under attack when fires raged through Yellowstone National Park, ultimately consuming more than 700,000 acres. The public was incensed when it learned that several of the fires had initially been allowed to burn and then got out of control.

Due to political pressure, prescription burning declined significantly after the Yellowstone fires. Nevertheless, it is still considered an effective fire-management tool by most forest experts, including the Forest Service. The problem today is that years of drought and insect damage have left many forests in such an inflammable state that it is too late for prescribed burns. At this point, the fires would be impossible to control.

The threat of forest fire has resulted in some measure of public support for salvage logging—the practice of clearing dead or dying trees from specific areas of forest. The Forest Service favors the practice because it reduces the level of combustible material in the forest. But most environmentalists oppose salvage logging, seeing

Right: *After the 1988 fires in Yellowstone, the Forest Service assessed the prescribed-fire policy and ultimately strengthened the guidelines.*

it as a euphemism for clearcutting—taking all trees, dead or alive, from a given area. While there is valid cause for concern, salvage logging can be environmentally sound if lumber companies will spend the necessary time and money to do it properly.

Experts agree that the removal of deadwood is critical to fire prevention and forest health. But the future of our western forests depends on long-term restorative action as well, says Neil Sampson, chairman of the National Commission on Wildfire Disasters and executive vice president of American Forests, an organization dedicated to improving and maintaining forest health.

American Forests has proposed legislation calling for such measures as thinning forests to improve green trees, converting forests to species that can succeed under climate stress, and employing some form of pest and disease control program.

Testifying before the House Agriculture Committee on June 30, 1992, Sampson said, "In order to achieve any of these actions, we need to recognize that this is not forest business as usual.... It is an emergency, and it needs to be treated as such, probably for a decade or longer."

Alice Quine

A FITTING TRIBUTE

At 3:10 p.m. on August 5, 1949, a plane began circling a forest fire in Mann Gulch, a remote wilderness area in the Montana mountains. On board was a 15-man crew of Forest Service Smokejumpers, most of them younger than 25. Within less than an hour, they were parachuting from the plane. The men were confident, accustomed to implementing the Forest Service's policy of putting out all wildfires as quickly as possible—no later than by 10 o'clock the morning after the fire started.

The fire at Mann Gulch appeared to be strictly routine. Then suddenly it exploded. The crew was caught in a blowup— "a catastrophic collision of fire, clouds, and winds." The only chance of escape lay in outracing the firestorm to reach a high ridge approximately 200 yards away.

Convinced that the race was futile, foreman Wag Dodge lit an "escape fire" in the grass directly ahead. After shouting for the crew to follow his lead, he lay down in the ashes of his fire, letting the main blaze pass over him. Whether the men did not understand Dodge or simply believed he had lost his mind will never be known. But instead of following him, they ran for the ridge. When it was all over, only Dodge and two

members of the crew had survived. The families of the dead boys filed suit against the Forest Service. The foreman's fire, they claimed, was responsible for the deaths of their sons.

Norman Maclean—a writer, teacher, and former Forest Service firefighter—saw the Mann Gulch fire while it was still burning. Haunted by the tragic deaths of the young men, he asked a question that stayed with him all his life: "Did any good, any good at all, come out of this?" In 1976, at the age of 74, Maclean set out to answer his question, to find out what had really happened at Mann Gulch that day.

Maclean's search dominated the last 14 years of his life. Young Men and Fire is his account of that search and the answers he found. Published in 1992, two years after Maclean's death, his book brings the story of Mann Gulch full circle. From that tragedy came new firefighting policies that now save the lives of countless men on the line. By finding meaning in their deaths, Maclean has paid tribute to the courageous young men who died. "For many of us," he said, "it would mean a great deal to know that, by our dying, we were often to be present in times of catastrophe helping to save the living from our deaths."

PEOPLE UNDER PRESSURE

Right: *In Papua New Guinea the government has set up "safe havens," where tribes can live free from interference.*

Below: *The San Bushmen of Botswana and Namibia survive by using their extensive knowledge of their desert home to exploit its sparse resources. Here they take ostrich eggs from a nest.*

Among the disparate interests clamoring for their part in the preservation of the biosphere, there is a group for whom conservation is a life-or-death matter—the indigenous people who inhabit the forests, deserts, and other shrinking wild regions at the center of conservation concerns. These people, living lives virtually unchanged for thousands of years, have frequently been ignored in the scramble to save the planet. Governments and businesses have often seen them as an impediment to development, and those wanting to exploit the land have made deliberate attempts to move indigenous people out of their traditional territories. This has led to their confinement in reservations and camps a fraction of the size of their tribal lands. Those people unwilling to move have been persecuted and even killed.

Indigenous people are as much a part of the modern world as those trying to help or exploit them—and it is their right to participate in any decisions concerning the conservation of their traditional territories. Conservationists have been almost as guilty as commercially interested parties in ignoring the wishes of the indigenous people themselves. There has been a tendency to romanticize them, seeing them as "noble savages," living lives of perfect innocence. This can lead to the worst sort of tourism, in which, as the tourist bus approaches, the tribal villagers shed their Western jeans and shirts, don a few ethnic accessories, and carry out "traditional" dances and rituals in return for handouts from the visitors.

Almost too late, many conservationists are realizing that indigenous people have

an enormous amount to teach the rest of the world about the last wildernesses. Their knowledge and skills are encyclopedic, and their age-old lifestyles are often sustainable in a way that puts the consumer societies of the developed world to shame. Without the participation of indigenous people, little progress is likely in the urgent struggle to conserve the planet's riches.

Many of the world's farmer-herders have developed cycles of seasonal activity that go back thousands of years, following patterns of food gathering that do not exhaust the land. In Niger the Tuareg nomadic farmer-herders of the Aïr Mountains graze their sheep, goats, and camels in wooded mountain valleys in the hot, dry season. When the rainy season approaches, they move the herds down to the surrounding plains. Half of the Tuareg people live in permanent villages. These people depend on small garden plots and on bartering produce for essentials that they do not produce themselves, such as salt, cereals, and dates.

In many cases, indigenous people are able to live sustainable lifestyles partly because there is so much land to support each individual. The Yanomami people of Brazil, for example, number about 9,000 and occupy about 36,300 square miles of rainforest. The total Indian population of modern Brazil is just 250,000—a twentieth of what it was at the time of the Spanish conquest.

The Yanomami grow much of their food on small plots in forest clearings, moving to new gardens every two or three years to allow the cultivated land to revert to forest and regenerate itself. The Yanomami move their villages every five to ten years. While four-fifths of their food comes from the plots they cultivate, they acquire much of their dietary protein and vitamins by hunting fish and game, as well as gathering nuts, fruits, and honey from the forest itself.

The Yanomami, like other Amazonian tribes, look upon the game they hunt and all the creatures of the forest as their ancestors. This reverence for the environment and for everything that lives in it is often found among indigenous people and helps to ensure that game is taken carefully, without waste. The Inuit hunter apologizes to the polar bear before killing it, addressing it respectfully as "uncle." The !Kung clan of San Bushmen will not hunt the elephant at all, because they consider its intelligence to be too close to their own.

This respect for the natural world often extends to the sympathetic exploitation of plants. The tribes of the Papua New Guinea highlands use over 600 plant species, most of them gathered in the wild. They build their houses from grasses and thatched leaves. Their traditional dress is made from bark, leaves, and twines of plant fiber. In the forest the tribespeople gather plants to make dyes, medicines, cosmetics, and poisons. In addition, they eat a bewilderingly large range of roots, fungi, leaves, fruits, and nuts. Tools, ropes, baskets, musical instruments, weapons, and ornaments all come from materials growing in the forest.

In Papua New Guinea, highlanders have been cultivating crop plots for nearly 10,000 years in fertile highland valleys. Their expert agricultural practices include the use of drained swamps and complex networks of carefully regulated drainage ditches and canals. By managing their water supplies,

Left: *The Inuit rely on hunting and fishing to sustain them in the frozen expanses of their northern home. Traditional hunting methods include a respect for prey rare among recreational hunters in the developed world.*

Left: *According to the Yanomami creation myth, the first people were transformed into the animals that inhabit the Brazilian forests today. Hunting is kept at a level that ensures the forest is never depleted of these ancestors.*

Right: *The dama gazelle is a rare species that has benefited from the nature reserve established in the Aïr Mountains of Niger. By helping the resident Tuareg people, the reserve's sponsors are also helping to protect rare animal species from the threat of overgrazing.*

Below: *Medicinal plants are commonly exploited by indigenous people. This young Solomon Islander has had his broken finger splinted with a raralu leaf.*

using rich mulches of decaying vegetable matter, and allowing short fallow periods, the highland tribes maintain a horticulture that is constantly replenished.

In strong contrast to Papua New Guinea highlanders, the San Bushmen of southern Africa are hunter-gatherers who have never cultivated crops or herded animals. Inhabiting desert lands where hunger, dehydration, and thirst can be rapid killers, the San have one of the highest protein intakes in the world. They are masters at surviving in this harsh terrain. The San are Africa's oldest human residents and may once have occupied the whole continent. Today they inhabit primarily parts of Botswana and Namibia that colonizers of many nationalities and races have found impossible to settle or exploit.

Highly skilled hunters, the San catch 80 species of animal, using bows and arrows, spears, snares, and traps. On the spear- and arrowheads, they use a poison taken from the pupae of flea beetles. While the men are hunting, the women and young children forage for tubers, fruits, and nuts. All of them may travel great distances in the course of a day in order to take advantage of the availability of water, shelter, and seasonal produce.

The !Kung people, one of the San tribes, live in small groups in Namibia and Botswana, moving between water holes and areas rich in food. However, very few San Bushmen still live a purely traditional life. Some of the young men go away to work for the South African army, while others have accepted the convenience of official settlement camps, with water on tap. Nearly all are influenced in some way by the outside world.

Other indigenous people have reached a similar crossover point between old and new styles of life. They have begun to take paid work, using money to buy food and goods sold by traders and in stores, rather than foraging daily. Conservationists should not be too quick to condemn such moves. Fresh water on tap, for example, is a huge asset to people used to a daily struggle to find water in conditions of drought.

The highlanders of Papua New Guinea, the Australian Aborigines, and, increasingly, the San Bushmen of southern Africa are all becoming more and more involved in the developed world. Political and economic pressures have been major factors, as governments cast a longing eye on extensive tribal lands and resources. Cultural pressures also play a part, as the younger generations grow impatient with tradition and begin to hanker after some of the aspects of the modern world brought home by contact with people outside the tribe. Despite having a foot in both worlds, these groups retain close links with the land, its plants, and its animals. Their communities are still repositories of extensive knowledge, although this, too, is under threat as the older generations die.

The Australian Aborigines, like the San, have inhabited their lands for thousands of years. Island hopping from Southeast Asia some 50,000 years ago, the first Australians radically altered the environment that greeted them. Using fire to clear the vegetation and as an aid to hunting, the Aborigines transformed forest regions into open savannalike plains, ensuring the supremacy of the fire-resistant eucalyptus tree and causing the extinction of many species that depended on plants that did not survive the fire treatment.

The damage that the first Aborigines inflicted on the land has been infinitely exceeded by their descendants' suffering at the hands of European settlers. It is remarkable that these people have been able to retain some of their rich cultural traditions despite racist victimization, the usurping of

Below: *Despite hundreds of years of persecution, some of Australia's Aborigines still preserve a life of astonishing integration with their vast, harsh environment.*

Right: *This Huli man from Papua New Guinea sports a wig made from the hair of family members.*

Below: *In Thailand, members of the Akha hill tribe work on a coffee and macadamia nut plantation. Such projects attempt to reconcile the demands of a market economy with the needs of indigenous people.*

important ritual lands and sites, and the institution of crudely inadequate reservations. One tradition that has been undergoing a revival among some Aborigine groups is the practice of foraging for "bush tucker," or wild foods. With reservation stores selling heavily sugared junk food, sliced white bread, and bottles of sweet tomato catsup, obesity and diabetes have become serious problems for listless reservation dwellers. However, tests have shown a remarkable turnaround in diabetic conditions and general health when traditional bush tucker is eaten instead of store-bought processed foods. The traditional diet is extremely varied, with a wide range of nuts, fruit, roots, and tubers, as well as animal protein from many different creatures. Some items are particularly nutritious: the billygoat plum may contain more vitamin C than any other known fruit.

The Aborigines have suffered from the exploitation of their native lands for commercial interests—to the extent that many of them are confined to reservations. But nowhere is the effect of environmental depredation more apparent than in the South American rainforests. Although the fate of the rainforests has a high media profile, the effect of their destruction on indigenous people is rarely discussed. As the trees are decimated so are countless insect species and everything else that thrives beneath the forest canopy, from birds, frogs, and snakes to monkeys, jaguars—and the people of forest tribes. Without the forests, the forest people become extinct; they are too dependent on the forest's resources and too few in numbers to survive in the outside world. In addition, diseases brought into the Amazon region by loggers, miners, and farmers have wiped out entire tribes that lack immunity to them.

Properly consulted and rewarded, forest tribes could help the outside world to reap the benefits of the forests' diversity, for the forests have far more wealth to give than the short-term profit obtainable from lumber. Even through simple agriculture local tribes can create needed foreign trade for debt-ridden governments while maintaining the habitats essential to their own survival. Rubber tappers have shown how to harvest wealth from constantly renewed resources. Some of the Kayapo Indians of Brazil do the same with Brazil nuts, which they harvest from single, scattered trees rather than plantations. They sell the oil, which they process themselves, to the "green" cosmetic industry.

The highlanders of Papua New Guinea have had similar success with growing and marketing organic coffee beans. Tribespeople gather the beans from trees growing in different parts of the forest. They then sell these beans, grown without the use of pesticides or fertilizers, to small foreign or-

ganizations that can find a ready market for organic coffee.

In areas where commercial coffee plantations have been established, there has often been strife between the entrepreneurs setting up the projects and the tribespeople who both own the land and work on the plantations. Because the tribespeople are not accustomed to regular hours of work, they may fail to gather coffee crops at the crucial time in the ripening cycle, spoiling the harvest. These people also feel that they receive too small a proportion of the profits in return for their labor.

This conflict shows the gulf of understanding that can exist between groups from the developed world and indigenous people. There is a fine line between cooperation and exploitation. We need to learn this distinction if we are to benefit from the vast human resources that exist in the few places where people still live in sympathy with their environment.

Duncan Brewer

PEOPLE OF THE AIR MOUNTAINS

The Aïr Mountains of Niger, which are home to about 5,000 Tuareg subsistence farmers and herders, are also inhabited by rare populations of ostrich, addax, and dama gazelle. The Aïr Mountains are of particular interest to conservationists because of their unspoiled state and regionally rare mammal populations. The Tuareg farmers and herders survive with their vegetable plots and seasonal grazing areas, causing negligible damage to the environment. Both water supplies and vegetation are sparse but sufficient for the small Tuareg population to survive most of the time. However, during periodic droughts, there is a damaging loss of crops and herd animals. Then the Tuareg migrate out of the region in large numbers, driven by lack of food as well as disease.

Formalized in 1988, *the Aïr and Ténéré National Nature Reserve is managed by the Nigerean Wildlife Service and has international sponsors such as the World Wide Fund for Nature and the Danish and Swiss governments. The reserve is nearly 30,000 square miles in area—almost four times the size of New Jersey. Unlike many other nature reserves, the Aïr project concerns itself with the problems of human as well as wildlife survival in this fragile environment, rightly recognizing that without an infrastructure that will protect the Tuareg inhabitants during periods of drought, the wildlife will suffer from overgrazing. The project has initiated development activities including health care and well digging, and the aim is for the Tuareg themselves to manage this huge protected area.*

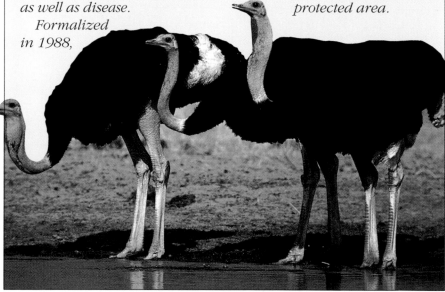

WILDLIFE IN THE GARDEN

Above: *Cottontails like grassy vegetation, but they need places of dense cover for shelter. Baby rabbits like this one may leave their nest at about two weeks old.*

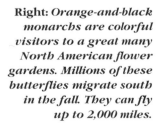

Right: *Orange-and-black monarchs are colorful visitors to a great many North American flower gardens. Millions of these butterflies migrate south in the fall. They can fly up to 2,000 miles.*

Throughout the United States, families are converting their backyards into refuges for wildlife and attracting a variety of insects, reptiles, birds, and mammals. Some people look out their windows to watch tiny hummingbirds sip nectar from bright red flowers or to glimpse chipmunks scurrying in and out of burrows. Others may catch sight of the electric blue tail of a young skink or spot a box turtle stealing a tasty tomato.

Anyone can turn a backyard into a mini-sanctuary for wildlife. You do not need to be an expert gardener or have a huge amount of land or money. A window box of flowers with a bowl of water and a dish of sunflower seeds will attract bees, butterflies, other insects, and some birds. If you have a small plot of land, you can welcome ground-feeding birds like mourning doves by planting grass, flowers, and shrubs. By coordinating your efforts with your neighbors, you can enlarge your wildlife habitat, providing corridors for rabbits and other mammalian visitors.

To make your yard inviting to animals, you need to provide four basic elements: food, water, shelter, and breeding sites. Different trees and shrubs supply berries, acorns, nuts, and other seeds for animals to eat, as well as places for birds and squirrels to nest. A flower bed lures butterflies and other insects, which birds catch to feed their young. A small pond may not only house frogs and tadpoles but also serve as a mecca for thirsty migratory birds or raccoons.

In planning your wildlife habitat, first take stock of what you already have. Do robins already come to dig worms out of

WILDLIFE & TOURISM

Above: *As the trend for more unusual vacations continues, tourists are becoming a familiar sight to the penguins of Antarctica.*

Right: *Tourists eager for photo opportunities often disturb the very wildlife they have come to observe.*

Governors

MASAI MARA GAME
KENYA

By the end of the decade, tourism will be the world's largest industry, with an enormous potential for changing our global environment. Each year, over 400 million people worldwide take international vacations, and the number is rising. Tourists are not only becoming more numerous, many of us are also becoming more demanding. We want more action, more adventure, and we want to go somewhere unspoiled, where conventional tourism has not yet stamped its indelible mark.

Responding to this demand, tour operators are offering a wider range of wildlife vacations for the 1990s than ever before. Whether it's watching humpback whales off Newfoundland, swimming with the sea lions of the Galápagos, or experiencing the "untamed" wilderness of Zimbabwe or Nepal, the wildlife-watching trend is rapidly growing. Some conservationists are heralding it as a potential force for environmental good. Certainly, it helps us to appreciate what we may lose if we continue to destroy the planet at the current pace. But we must plan now if wildlife tourism is to have a positive impact on the environment—or at least if it is to avoid the environmental abuse of traditional tourism.

Tourism must become sustainable—that is, it must not take from the environment more than can be naturally replaced or alter a habitat beyond repair. Past evidence offers little cause for optimism, however: the impact of mass tourism on the world's most popular vacation spots has been disastrous and, tragically, irreversible.

In the Alps, hundreds of square miles of forest have been cleared to make way for

Below: *Land iguanas obtain nourishment from abundant cacti.*

This policy meant that no facilities had to be built in the national park. It also provided an income for the boat operators and guides. Most important, it meant that not only would the guides act as wardens, controlling the tourists, but they would also add to the visitors' enjoyment by providing in-depth information about the islands' wildlife. The system works very well, and it has been copied in parks and reserves around the world.

The Galápagos National Park covers approximately 3,000 square miles, or 97 percent of the land area of the islands. The only land excluded is land that was already occupied by settlers in 1969. The human inhabitants of the Galápagos adjusted quite quickly to the idea of not disturbing the native wildlife. Most were happy to benefit from the income generated by the gradually increasing number of visitors. But the conservationists have faced other problems, such as controlling the introduced animals and plants that were threatening native species. These animals include dogs, cats, rats, house mice, goats, pigs, donkeys, horses, cattle, and even scarab beetles and fire ants. Some will never be eradicated on all the islands, due to a combination of the rugged terrain and the sheer survival skills of the animals themselves.

There have been some successes, however. Dogs and pigs have been greatly reduced. Goats, the most destructive of all the exotics, have been eliminated from five islands, but their astonishing reproductive potential is well illustrated on Pinta Island. Three goats were released there, as a future food supply, by fishermen in 1957. By 1968 the population reached 10,000 to 15,000, and a mere three years after that the total soared to around 25,000. Fortunately, park service personnel have managed to eliminate most of the goats, and the vegetation is growing back steadily. But it is a tough and costly battle that is far from over.

The native vegetation of the Galápagos is just as special as the islands' many unique animal species. Yet these plants are threatened not only by the introduced animals, but also by the steady spread of plants and

114

trees brought by the settlers in the last century. Some of the intruders are food plants, some are ornamental or medicinal plants, and others are trees that provide building materials. Seeds, too, have been brought in accidentally. All told, there are more than 260 introduced plant species.

The introduced plants are generally more successful than the native species, starving them of sunlight, water, and nutrients. Some of these are extremely damaging. Lantana, which was brought to Floreana Island to beautify a family garden, now covers almost eight square miles, its seeds dispersed by the native Darwin's finches and by introduced rats. It forms dense thickets and prevents the endangered dark-rumped petrel from entering its nesting burrows.

Passion fruit vines climb native trees and block out the sun, guava trees have formed large forests covering more than 150 square miles, while red quinine trees are spread-

ing through the unique Miconia vegetation zone in the highlands of Santa Cruz Island. In most cases, it is very difficult to eradicate introduced plants. As with the alien animals, the best that can probably be hoped for is to contain their spread.

There is, however, good news to balance this catalog of problems. Two decades of captive breeding of reptiles by biologists, helped by park personnel, have been strikingly successful. More than 1,000 captive-reared giant tortoises have been released on their ancestral islands, and most of the 11 surviving subspecies of these famous creatures are being reestablished. Unfortunately, little can be done for the Pinta Island tortoise, since only one male, nicknamed "Lonesome George," survives. Of special note is the Hood Island race, which has a saddle-shaped carapace. Only two elderly males and 11 females remained in the 1960s, and these were so widely dispersed that they never met. Now, some 250 young

Above: *Lumbering and helpless, giant tortoises were sitting targets for hungry sailors and settlers. They enjoy a safer future today, assuming a star role in the many tourist attractions of the Galápagos.*

Left: *In the cloud forests of Santa Cruz Island, tree-dwelling vegetation decorates the branches. Some two-thirds of the plant species on the Galápagos cannot be found anywhere else in the world.*

tortoises have been returned to the island, where they should soon begin breeding. Biologists at the station have achieved similarly promising results with land iguanas, breeding and reintroducing three endangered subspecies.

In the last century, sealers almost wiped out the Galápagos fur seals, but thanks to strict protection in recent decades, these animals number about 40,000 today. Pacific green turtles are doing well, too, with thousands returning each year to lay their eggs on pristine Galápagos beaches. There was a scare during the early 1970s when a Japanese refrigerator ship arrived and, with local assistance, collected large numbers. But the Darwin station director at the time, Peter Kramer, persuaded the Ecuadorian

government to ban this commercial exploitation indefinitely.

Recently, two new difficulties have surfaced. When the national park was established, planners estimated that up to 12,000 tourists a year could visit without harming the environment. There were virtually none at the time, but numbers increased during the 1970s as the wonders of the Galápagos were publicized. By 1984 about 20,000 people were coming every year. Then, suddenly, there was a rise to over 40,000 in 1988. The figure is now nudging 50,000.

The authorities are now trying to make this the upper limit, mainly by refusing to issue any more boat licenses. But the local Ecuadorian population is expanding, and there is a demand to allow more boats in

Below: *Penguins dart and twist as they chase a school of panicked prey. Scientists are very concerned that a slump in the Galápagos fish stocks may put entire food chains at risk.*

order to provide more jobs. The park has so far absorbed visitors without significant evidence of stress, but at some point the environment will suffer and the quality of the experience will be degraded for the visitors.

A bigger problem, however, is that many people have been arriving on the islands from the mainland of Ecuador in the hope of exploiting the tourist boom. Today some 12,000 people live there, mainly on Santa Cruz and San Cristobal islands, but the land available is strictly limited and therefore very expensive. Pressure is mounting to release some land from the national park to accommodate these people, many of whom do not understand the fragile link between conservation and tourism.

An additional alarming trend is the over-exploitation of marine resources. Unlike the land, the waters of the Galápagos were not protected until the formation of a 27,000-square-mile Marine Resources Reserve in 1986. This covers all of the archipelago, up to 15 nautical miles offshore. In 1992 the outer limit was extended to 80 miles for foreign fishing vessels. But because of all the different agencies claiming jurisdiction—including those involved with the law of the sea, defense, tourism, fisheries, and development—it has proved difficult to agree on how to regulate activities within the reserve, and protective policies are hard to enforce. For example, the large groupers known locally as bacalao are much sought after by fishermen, but catches have steadily declined in weight and size of fish. Today, 70 percent of the bacalao landed are immature. Fishermen are also taking lobsters below the legal size, including females with eggs. Nor are closed seasons fully observed.

Foreign fishing vessels, mostly Japanese, Korean, and Taiwanese, are now reportedly waiting outside the exclusion zone, while local or mainland-based boats fish on their behalf. The development of large-scale commercial fishing threatens whales and

dolphins, sea lions, and fur seals, as well as a host of seabirds such as tropicbirds, boobies, frigatebirds, and the rare Galápagos penguins and flightless cormorants.

Ecuador has now enacted most of the laws necessary to control exploitation of the Galápagos waters. However, the Galápagos National Park Service has neither the money nor the personnel to take more than token action, and the navy's pair of 30-knot patrol vessels can do little in an area of 27,000 square miles. Meanwhile, divers report that hammerhead and other sharks are hard to find in areas where they were once plentiful. This may be just the tip of the iceberg.

The Charles Darwin Foundation is pressuring the Ecuadorian government to set up a properly funded management authority for the marine reserve. It is lobbying for prompt action to stop the plunder of marine resources, which are just as significant as the terrestrial wildlife of the archipelago. For if the degradation of the Galápagos is allowed to continue it will have tragic consequences not only for this island paradise but for the natural world as a whole.

Nigel Sitwell

Above: *The waved albatross breeds almost exclusively on Hood Island in the Galápagos.*

Overleaf: *Marine iguanas throng the Galápagos coasts— both above and below the hissing surf.*

WILDLIFE
& CONSERVATION
ORGANIZATIONS

It is usually the dramatic conservation stories that hit the news, such as an attempt to rescue an endangered animal. But we hear little of the conservationists themselves and even less of the laws that govern their activities.

In this section we first look at conservation work in Belize, where wildlife as a whole has benefited from attempts to protect the jaguar. We then trace the growth of the National Audubon Society, from its beginnings as an organization founded for the conservation of birds to one that is now concerned with all aspects of the environment. On a local scale is the Mississippi River Revival, one of the nation's many grass-roots groups whose efforts prove that concerned individuals can make a difference.

We also provide an overview of the laws that help to protect the world's wildlife, followed by an in-depth look at the National Wildlife Federation—one of the largest conservation organizations in the United States. Finally, we offer a report on Greenpeace—one of the world's highest-profile conservation groups.

Above left: *Trained conservationists must combine forces with local people to make conservation projects an ongoing success.*

Above: *Observation is as important as intervention in the monitoring of rare or threatened species.*

Left: *1992 was not an easy year for the International Whaling Commission, and it is vital that conservation organizations continue to campaign for the world's beleaguered marine mammals.*

JAGUARS & THE JUNGLE

Above: *In the Belizean forest the praying mantis lurks on a bougainvillea while waiting to snatch prey.*

Far right: *This young jaguar relieves the irritation of teething by gnawing on a branch.*

Right: *The deadly fer-de-lance consumes a frog headfirst. After such a meal, it is some time before the snake needs to eat again.*

As it stands in the undergrowth by a forest trail, the stocky body and large head of the jaguar are all but invisible. Its golden coat, dappled with black rosettes, melts into the early morning shadows and the light filtering through the leaves. Cautiously, it emerges and walks down the track with a heavy, almost ungainly step before disappearing again into the rainforest.

The jaguar typically inhabits lowland jungles near rivers but has been seen in the mountains of Bolivia and Peru. Its range once stretched from the United States south to Uruguay and Argentina, but its numbers are now greatly reduced. Since 1973 it has been classified as vulnerable to extinction.

Hunting has played a part in the jaguar's decline, for its coat has been prized for thousands of years, by ancient Mayan priests as well as modern furriers. Before trade in this animal's fur was banned, up to 39,000 jaguars were killed each year. Some hunting continues illegally today. But the greatest threat to the jaguar comes from the clearing of its forest habitat for timber and to make space for farms and human settlements.

It is hard to assess how critical the jaguar's situation has become because no one knows the size of former or current populations. Why has this big cat been studied so little? The main reason is that its forest habitats are often hard for researchers to reach, and long-term projects have been made more dangerous by the political instability of many of its native countries. The jaguar's habits make study even more difficult: this solitary beast has a large territory and tends to hunt at dusk and dawn. All in all, it is not surprising that until 10 years ago very little was known about the lifestyle of this beautiful creature.

The situation has been slowly changing, and in some places genuine efforts are now being made to study and protect the jaguar. In the small Central American country of Belize, there is still a healthy jaguar population. In 1984 the Cockscomb Basin Jaguar Preserve was opened in woodland previously logged for timber. Other forest reserves have also been established, and the country now has an impressive and varied network of conservation areas.

In the forests where it lives, the jaguar is at the top of the food chain. It eats just about anything it can catch, varying its diet depending on the season of the year and its habitat. Peccaries are a favorite food, but these bristly-haired piglike mammals can be extremely fierce. The jaguar picks off any young or old peccaries that stray, but it is unwilling to tackle an entire herd. Frequently, it opts for smaller, easier prey animals such as anteaters, iguanas, pacas, and agoutis, although this means hunting more often. Armadillos are also featured prominently in the 80 or so recorded prey species. According to Melanie Watt, an expert on the Belizean jaguar, it has been reported eating "everything from avocados to anacondas."

In Belize the jaguar is known as *el tigre,* but its true name comes from a South American Tupi-Guarani word—*yaguara*—which means "wild beast that overcomes its prey in a single bound." This is an exact descrip-

Above: *The limpid-eyed margay is the smallest of Belize's spotted cats. Little is known about the habits of this shy, nocturnal creature.*

The jaguar shares its territory with many other cat species. Ocelots, pumas, margays, and jaguarundis are found with jaguars in many of Belize's forest reserves. Moreover, the ranges of male jaguars may overlap; scent and claw marks are used to warn off intruders and avoid potentially fatal fights.

The most frequently hunted cat in Latin America is the ocelot, or "tiger cat," as it is known in Belize. It can weigh more than 30 pounds and has a beautiful striped and spotted coat, making it a coveted prize even though it is a threatened species.

It is extremely difficult to identify animals in the rainforest, and when distance makes it hard to guess size, an ocelot may be identified by hopeful eyes as a jaguar.

It is even harder to tell an ocelot from a margay. The margay is the smallest spotted cat in Belize and the one about which the least is known. This arboreal cat is gracefully built and slimmer than the ocelot, with a longer tail. It is hunted for its fur and is also trapped for the pet market.

Protecting jaguars and other cats is important in Belize, since it relies heavily on tourism for its national income. Its commitment to conservation has attracted many thousands of visitors to its nature reserves. Not only is Belize safeguarding its tourist industry, but it is also saving the forest and the many creatures besides jaguars that live there. Areas that would probably have been cleared for citrus or banana plantations will now be left in their natural state.

A contributor to the conservation efforts has been the Programme for Belize (PFB), which was founded in 1988 with a grant from the Massachusetts Audubon Society. Its aim has been to help solve the problems that arise when the needs of people conflict with those of their environment. Much of Belize's land is privately owned, and the PFB's initial plan was to buy a large stretch of suitable forest and protect it forever using a land management plan. The idea was to

tion of the way it hunts. In relation to its size, the jaguar has the most powerful jaws in the cat family. It kills by biting through the back of its prey's neck or skull, but if it is hunting a large animal it leaps onto its prey's back. It then knocks its victim off-balance by pulling the animal's head to the side with its paw.

There are many stories of unprovoked jaguar attacks on humans—although compared with the other big cats, it does not have a big reputation as a man-eater. The jaguar is more likely to come into conflict with local people if it develops a taste for cattle. This occurs most frequently with injured jaguars. In normal circumstances, the jaguar is reluctant to cross open ground, so livestock are safe unless they are kept by the edge of the forest. Jaguars have often been blamed for cattle theft when the culprit was human.

employ local people to use the land in ways that were both sustainable and harmless to the resident wildlife.

Money was raised in the United States and Britain, and in 1990, some 170 square miles of forest in the Rio Bravo area were purchased, forming the core of the Rio Bravo Conservation and Management Area. Adjoining this is another 200-square-mile area that is privately owned but managed along similar lines. An additional area of about 145 square miles was donated by Coca-Cola in two parts, in 1990 and 1992.

The various areas in the northwest corner of Belize fit together like pieces of a jigsaw puzzle. Much of the land is prime tropical forest, filled with monkeys, tapirs, pumas, jaguars, peccaries, and countless birds, including toucans, motmots, and king vultures. Many areas have been selectively logged for years, but these stretches of secondary forest are still lush and beautiful. The reserve has been divided into zones. Zone 1 areas are left completely wild; zone 2 areas are

set aside for wildlife observation and research. Zone 3 land will eventually be harvested selectively for its wood, medicinal plants, and chicle (used in chewing gum), while zone 4 land will be used for tourist facilities and archaeological research. The income from harvests and tourism will subsidize the cost of running the reserve.

Grants from the United States now fund three rangers and a research station manager. These positions are important because people have been found illegally setting up home inside the reserve and growing crops there, and chicle is being stolen from some trees. Ruined Mayan temples that have been discovered in the reserve must also be protected until they can be properly explored.

Cooperating with local people in running a reserve can be difficult, but it works well most of the time. Belizeans take pride in their natural heritage, and the level of lit-

Above: *Along Belize's coast, a rare manatee cruises through the warm waters it prefers. This completely aquatic mammal benefits from protected marine areas.*

Left: *Exotic plant species such as the black orchid abound in the lush humidity of Belize's tropical forests.*

127

eracy is high, so it is easy to publicize the work of the reserves. Belize is about the size of New Hampshire, but its population is only 250,000, so it does not suffer from the overcrowding that often drives people to clear rainforests in other parts of Central and South America. It is also a very stable country politically, which helps.

The Community Baboon Sanctuary is a good example of local involvement in conservation. In 1985, 11 landowners pledged to manage their lands to benefit the declining populations of the howler monkey, known in Belize as the baboon. They left strips of forest on the property borders and did not cut down the fruit trees the monkey prefers. Where roads and clearings separated trees, they even installed aerial walkways. Soon, visitors began to arrive.

More than 100 landowners from different villages are now involved, and some people offer bed and breakfast to tourists.

Above: *Belize's invertebrates, such as the exquisite malachite butterfly, benefit from various conservation projects that preserve land from clearance.*

Right: *The female black howler monkey lacks the bony chamber in the throat that amplifies the male's astonishing calls.*

The villagers have gained a steady income, while visitors get a rare glimpse of rural Belize. At times during the day, and especially at dawn and dusk, the howler monkeys steal the show with their amazing cacophony; the sound of rival troops bellowing at each other can be heard up to a mile away. Thanks to the sanctuary, from 1985 to1988 the local howler population increased from about 840 animals to more than 1,000.

Unfortunately, the Community Baboon Sanctuary covers only a small area, and howler monkeys elsewhere must take their chances with an enemy far more deadly than any natural predator—forest clearance.

Large reserves, however, can sustain vast numbers of species. The Rio Bravo Conservation Area is just one of several large reserves in Belize. In the Cockscomb Basin Jaguar Preserve, which was set up to preserve jaguars, there are also thousands of other species. The Mountain Pine Ridge Reserve is now the only place in Belize where

easily recognized by their long, overhanging snout. Since the tapir is Belize's national animal, it is especially important to preserve those populations surviving in the wild.

In 1990 the World Wildlife Fund warned that the jaguar could be extinct by the end of the century. The work of both scientists and the government of Belize may have stabilized its decline there just in time. Fortunately, the jaguar breeds rapidly in the right conditions, and populations are then able to recover. The growth of eco-tourism in Belize is a strong weapon in the battle to preserve the jaguars that are left.

One of the difficulties of promoting visits to rainforest reserves, however, is the probability that the tourists will not see any big, glamorous animals. Belize cannot compete with safari tours on the plains of Africa, where the animals live in the open. Instead, it can offer a sense of true adventure—the thrill of following tracks, of smelling the forest, hearing strange noises, and seeing shapes in every shadow. For a lucky few, there will also be the magical moment when they look back along a trail and their gaze is met by a pair of inquisitive bright yellow eyes.

Sarah Foster

Left: *Although trade in ocelot fur is banned under international law, a certain amount of poaching still threatens this endangered cat.*

Below: *The keel-billed toucan is one of the many colorful species that make a visit to Belize attractive to an increasing number of eco-tourists.*

rare orange-breasted falcons can be found. The Crooked Tree Wildlife Sanctuary—a wetland area—is important as a feeding station for birds. At the Hol Chan Marine Reserve, which is off the coast of Ambergris Cay, visitors can peer at Belize's barrier reef through diving masks or glass-hulled boats. The Half Moon Cay Reserve, located on the outer reaches of the reef, contains many seabirds, including a colony of 4,000 red-footed boobies.

There is still a need for ongoing conservation work in Belize. A team of scientists from London's Natural History Museum has been surveying an area in the Upper Raspaculo region in the Maya Mountains. It is the first time the mammals of this area have been studied, and a great number of species have been identified from sightings, tracks, and droppings. These include southern river otters and the rare Baird's tapir. Tapirs live on a diet of many different leaves and can weigh up to 660 pounds. They are

FOR BIRDS & MORE

Above: *The showy lady's slipper is one of many rare orchids that have benefited from the National Audubon Society's efforts to protect it.*

Right: *Saving the great egret was the National Audubon Society's first success, and this bird became a symbol of all the Society's activities.*

The National Audubon Society, named after John James Audubon, the pioneer artist and naturalist of the 19th century, has always been linked in the popular mind with birds. And indeed, when the organization was incorporated in 1905, under the name National Association of Audubon Societies, its primary mission was the conservation of birds. At issue was the slaughter of thousands of egrets and other plumed waders for their feathers, which were used to decorate women's hats.

The battle to save the egrets from extinction was waged in legislative halls and courtrooms. Before the destruction of the birds for the millinery trade was stopped, two Audubon wardens were murdered on the birds' nesting grounds in Florida. This galvanized public support, and the birds gained legal protection. The great egret became the National Audubon Society's emblem—a symbol of its first success.

Audubon has continued to fight for the passage of major laws affording protection to birds of all kinds—not only laws safeguarding them from slaughter for their plumage, but also laws protecting all migratory species other than game birds; laws banning the use of dangerous pesticides and toxic substances in general; and laws requiring environmental impact statements before any ecologically significant habitat is threatened by destruction. The scope of the Society's activities extends far beyond bird protection and now includes virtually all aspects of the environment's plight—from saving endangered and threatened animals and plants and protecting critical habitats, to promoting the sensible use of nonre-

Above: *With the National Audubon Society's help, the Atlantic puffin has now returned to nest at breeding sites in Maine.*

Below: *The Society helps educate youngsters, like these children facing a striped skunk, about the value of conservation.*

newable resources, combating acid rain and the depletion of the ozone layer, and trying to avoid or lessen the greenhouse effect.

The National Audubon Society operates with a full-time staff of over 300, including scientists, naturalists, educators, and lobbyists. It administers a network of more than 80 sanctuaries that together comprise over a quarter million acres. These sanctuaries protect precious wetlands, forests, grasslands, and even suburban areas, as well as the many species of plants and animals that live in them. Through the new Sharing the Earth program, some of these protected lands serve as living laboratories where scientists are studying ways in which large human populations and wildlife areas can coexist in harmony.

The National Audubon Society has over 500 local chapters in all 50 states and more than 600,000 members. Its grass-roots support allows it to mobilize large numbers of well-informed activists on the national level and also respond to local problems.

Members are kept abreast of important conservation issues through *Audubon*, the Society's award-winning magazine. In re-

turn for pledging to send two letters and make two phone calls to their representative in Congress, members can also receive the *Audubon Activist*, the Society's fact-filled monthly newsjournal. The *Audubon Activist* provides up-to-the-minute information on what Congress, federal agencies, and private companies are doing, or not doing, and how this will affect the environment. The *Activist* also publishes tips on how members can help fight global problems like the greenhouse effect and acid rain; a recent issue identified products that contain environmentally hazardous chemicals and are commonly used in the home. At longer intervals, the Society also releases its influential and authoritative Audubon Policy Reports, which cover a variety of environmental issues.

The programs of the National Audubon Society are as varied as are the threats to our global environment. The Society has taken a leading role in the fight to save the Arctic National Wildlife Refuge in northwestern Alaska. This pristine wilderness is, at 8,900,000 acres, the largest in the entire national wildlife refuge system. It is the home of grizzly, polar, and black bears, muskoxen, caribou, and hundreds of other tundra- and forest-dwelling species, but it is currently in danger from companies that want to explore it for oil.

Another battle is underway to save the South Platte River in Colorado and Nebraska—a vital resting and feeding place for migratory birds on their way to and from their northern nesting grounds. This river is threatened by damming and diversion. Another river in Nebraska was saved; 76 miles of the Niobrara have been designated a Scenic River by Congress, largely through the efforts of Audubon staff and members.

Yet another program, one that relies heavily on talented local support, is an effort to preserve the unique habitat and wildlife of the Edwards Plateau in Texas,

Left: *The Arctic National Wildlife Refuge in Alaska is the largest unit in the national wildlife refuge system—larger than the states of Massachusetts, Connecticut, and Rhode Island combined.*

home to some of the 700 species presently on the U.S. endangered species list and the source of drinking water for several large cities. "Listen to the Sound" was a series of hearings on Long Island Sound, intended to coordinate efforts to clean up this overcrowded, overused, and badly polluted body of water. The plight of the Adirondack wilderness in upstate New York has also attracted Audubon's attention.

An innovative scheme that relies heavily on grass-roots support is the Society's Adopt-a-Forest program, in which members fan out to map and monitor specific forest tracts, preparing inventories of species and watching for signs of environmental stress. The information the volunteers collect is relayed to the Washington office, where major concerns are taken up with Congress and the U.S. Fish and Wildlife Service.

Energy issues are another concern of Audubon. It has formed the Solar Brigade, a nationwide effort in support of the use of solar power as an alternative energy source, and is actively campaigning for the closing of nuclear power stations. The Society's new headquarters, in a carefully renovated building in New York City, serves as a model in this environmentally conscious age. The building uses less than half the energy consumed by a typical office building but emits significantly smaller amounts of greenhouse gases. Fully 80 percent of the material used in daily office operations is recycled. The goal is to inspire city officials and the public to start doing business in this cheaper yet environmentally cleaner way.

On the international front, an Audubon team has joined with Russian scientists to establish a system for monitoring acid rain. The Society is working with other conservation groups, both here and in Russia, to set up a Bering Sea international park. It is also working with environmental groups and governments around the world to meet the goals outlined at the 1992 Earth Summit in Rio de Janeiro. The National Audubon Society watches to make sure that interna-

Above: *Once threatened with extinction from pesticides, the bald eagle is now staging a comeback, thanks to efforts of the National Audubon Society as well as other organizations.*

tional treaties banning trade in endangered species are respected.

The Society has always been active in education. It operates six nature centers around the country, where both adults and children learn about natural history and conservation. The oldest of these, the Audubon Camp of Maine at Hog Island in Muscongus Bay, opened its doors in 1935. That first year, Roger Tory Peterson was one of the bird instructors.

Audubon Adventures brings the cause of conservation to more than 17,000 elementary school classes, reaching over 550,000 students, each of whom receives Audubon Adventures' newspaper. This success has been due in no small measure to the active support of local chapters and members.

Recently, the U.S. Department of Education granted the Audubon Science Institute

$210,000 to develop a national strategy to integrate environmental issues and sound science education. This program, designed for teachers in junior high schools, now reaches over 10,000 students annually.

The Society's award-winning television series "World of Audubon" reaches out to Americans of all ages, bringing the Audubon message to millions of viewers in their own homes. Recent National Audubon Society specials have included programs on coral reefs, the beleaguered wildlife of Hawaii, the national wildlife refuge system, the wetlands along the Intracoastal Waterway, and population and the environment, comparing a family living in Manhattan and one living in Madagascar.

With all its various activities, the National Audubon Society has not forgotten the birds that brought it into being. It maintains its

Right: *Since many of its breeding lakes have been polluted by acid rain, the common loon may soon become an endangered species. The Society is fighting to prevent this loss.*

Left: *The preservation of wetlands, such as this rich freshwater marsh in the northern United States, has always been one of the National Audubon Society's major concerns.*

long-standing commitment to the conservation of birds through its magazine *American Birds,* which provides seasonal reports on the status of all species, whether they are at risk or not. As part of its wide-ranging approach, *American Birds* recently published a detailed article on the threat posed by hydrodevelopment at James Bay in Ontario, a key migratory stopping place.

Most Audubon chapters have a strong representation of birders. The Christmas Bird Count, an annual bird census that is probably the Society's best-known activity, now involves more than 40,000 participants, who conduct more than 1,600 counts each year in all 50 states, every Canadian province, tropical America, and the Pacific. The results of the Christmas Bird Count are published every year in *American Birds*.

The Society's widely imitated Birdathon is a yearly fund-raising event in which birders ask sponsors to pledge a donation for every bird species they can find on one special day during the spring migration. The proceeds usually run to millions of dollars.

One of Audubon's greatest successes in recent years has been the reestablishment of the Atlantic puffin on Eastern Egg Rock in Muscongus Bay, Maine. Researchers are now trying again on nearby Seal Island.

On the West Coast, the Society recently acquired Tenmile Creek Audubon Sanctuary, near Coos Bay in Oregon. This reserve, which contains unspoiled coastal temperate rainforest, is the home of a healthy population of the marbled murrelet, a species of seabird that flies inland and nests in undisturbed forest. With its total U.S. population estimated at only about 9,000, the marbled murrelet was placed on the threatened list late in 1992.

Although birds are no longer Audubon's sole focus, they—like humans and all living things on this planet—are the beneficiaries of the Society's efforts to safeguard the Earth's fragile ecosystems and clean up the environment. Wild birds and their changing status form a valuable early-warning system, letting us know when there is something out of order in the natural world around us. They will always be an important part of the planning and programs of the National Audubon Society.

John Farrand, Jr.

REVIVAL ON THE RIVER

Right: *MRR's authentic birchbark canoe is symbolic of the group's commitment to strong ties with the Native American community and to maintaining the tradition of the river, linking the past to the present. In this photo, the canoe leads MRR's 10th anniversary flotilla.*

At a time when idealism is often forgotten, the Mississippi River Revival (MRR) provides a welcome reminder. This grassroots group has been working to restore the Mississippi River since 1981, spreading the word that people can make a difference, no matter how severe the problem. And this 2,350-mile long waterway is indeed a problem. Cited as one of the 10 most endangered rivers in the country, the Mississippi is plagued by everything from industrial discharge and nuclear waste to oil spills and untreated sewage. Nevertheless, MRR members believe that the river can come back, and their spirit is contagious.

With its regional office in Minneapolis, the group's efforts have centered on the upper Mississippi. "But the dream of MRR has always been to work for one river, from the headwaters to the Gulf," says Roger Aiken, the regional treasurer. As such, MRR sees itself as part of a network of groups spanning the river, with each group doing what it does best and supporting the efforts of the others.

One of the things MRR does best is mobilize people to clean up the river. MRR members have collected some 1,000 tons of garbage from the waters and shores over the last 12 years. Although the work is serious, the spirit is festive, with friends and neighbors meeting on the river to form a flotilla of canoes, johnboats, and other watercraft. Cleanup campaigns are marked by singing, laughing, and an astonishing assortment of trash. A typical haul may include everything from plastic bags and styrofoam cups to a tractor tire or even the rusted frame of a car.

For cleanups as well as other projects, local chapters can make use of the Dream Keeper—MRR's 26-foot authentic birchbark canoe. This hand-crafted boat is a replica of the 18th-century voyageur canoes used by French fur traders, which in turn were modeled on Native American canoes.

With the Dream Keeper, MRR brings a bit of history to the river, linking the past to the present and demonstrating the group's commitment to strong ties with the Native American community. So it seems fitting that for its maiden voyage, the Dream Keeper led MRR's 10th anniversary flotilla in the summer of 1990. Starting at the headwaters in Bemidji, Minnesota, and traveling down to Dubuque, Iowa, the flotilla covered over 600 miles, stopping at communities along the way for cleanups, concerts, and river displays.

The colorful flotillas attract attention and help drum up support for the Mississippi. But MRR engages in other types of endeavors as well. Group staff members Amy Middleton and Paul Schollmeier conducted a water-quality survey that ultimately led to the discovery of a plume of suspended solids—pollution that was traced to the city-owned Minneapolis Water Works. MRR turned the case over to Citizens for a Better Environment, which sued the city in 1991

Below: *Once the main means of transportation along the Mississippi, steamboats were phased out after the Civil War. But they still operate on the river today—as excursion boats.*

Right: *An enormous amount of trash pollutes the Mississippi. MRR members collect tons of it each year.*

Below: *The Mississippi is the second-longest river in the United States. Starting at Lake Itasca in northwestern Minnesota, it flows all the way to the Gulf of Mexico.*

under the Clean Water Act. The case was settled out of court a year later, with the city agreeing to upgrade its drinking water treatment plant and help fund environmental projects for the Mississippi. MRR was one of nine projects funded, receiving $2,000 for a festival and river cleanup.

While cleanup continues to be a major focus, MRR is also committed to education. In an attempt to reach children, the group launched its Riverschool project in the spring of 1992. The pilot program was conducted at the Dowling School in Minneapolis, where MRR volunteers presented fourth-graders with songs and stories about the Mississippi, a historical perspective of the river, and information about alternative energy. As the grand finale, the children were treated to a trip on the river in MRR's Dream Keeper.

The participants in this program had many reasons for donating their time and expertise, but a feeling for the Mississippi seemed to be the common thread. Jane Curry, a professional storyteller and the author of a book about riverboat pilots, summed up her motivation with this statement: "I have a fondness for the river, and I love to tell stories. I saw this as a way for the children to connect with the river and get a feel for its richness and lore."

Volunteers also form the backbone of MRR's River Watch program, which is similar to many river-monitoring programs in the United States. Local citizens are encouraged to form groups, "adopt" a stretch of river, and choose a project to help protect it. Projects range from trash cleanups and tree planting to water-quality testing and pollution-source monitoring. In addition to

benefiting the river, the projects serve as learning experiences for the participants. For example, river watch groups can learn to monitor water quality by identifying the insects in the water. MRR provides an illustrated "insect card" that correlates species with water quality. The presence of mayflies, for instance, indicates good water quality, while an abundance of blackflies means that water quality is poor.

River watchers also monitor the water by noting certain colors and odors, then consulting a chart that links water conditions with possible causes. For example, a yellowish coating on the riverbed may be the result of polluted water draining from a coal mine, while a musky odor may indicate untreated sewage or livestock waste.

With river watchers doing their part to protect the Mississippi, MRR comes one step closer to achieving its dream. But the group has no illusions about the time and effort the process will take. What it does have is patience and dedication. "The Mississippi is a legacy that needs to be protected," says Roger Aiken. "I guess you might say we see ourselves as keepers of the river."

Alice Quine

TWAIN ON THE MISSISSIPPI

Mark Twain took his name from the Mississippi; in return, he gave the river lasting fame. Back in the days of the steamboats, mark twain *was river jargon for "two fathoms." At that depth, it was safe for a boat to move ahead. Samuel Clemens adopted Mark Twain as his pen name when he embarked upon his career as a writer. Having spent two years as an apprentice and two years as a licensed pilot, he knew the language of the river as well as anyone who worked on it. And he made the Mississippi a prominent feature in some of his greatest pieces of literature.*

With Tom Sawyer *and* Huckleberry Finn, *Twain recreated his own boyhood during the 1840s in Hannibal, Missouri, a small town on the Mississippi. In that time and place, the arrival of a steamboat was cause for tremendous excitement. The boats not only brought news of the world to the isolated villages that lined the river, they also brought a glimpse of glamour. These "floating palaces," as they were called, were elaborately furnished and decorated in the grandiose style of the era's finest hotels. Then, too, there were the showboats, with actors bringing melodrama and vaudeville to the banks of the river.*

Twain's great affection for the river is clearly apparent when he depicts it through the eyes of Tom and Huck—his best-known fictional characters. But it is in nonfiction that the author reveals his deepest feelings about the river.

In Life on the Mississippi, *Twain recorded his experiences as an apprentice pilot, giving readers a graphic picture of the arduous effort involved. In order to qualify for his pilot's license, he had to memorize more than 1,200 miles of the lower Mississippi—every sandbar, snag, channel, and obstruction. Although he viewed the enormity of the task with a dread akin to despair, Twain persevered. "The face of the water, in time, became a wonderful book . . . ," he said. "And it was not a book to be read once and thrown aside, for it had a new story to tell every day."*

INTERNATIONAL WILDLIFE LAW

Right: *The 1961 Antarctic Treaty aims to protect the vast, ownerless southern continent but lacks the power to enforce its own well-intentioned rules.*

Below: *It is essential that any treaty aimed at conserving a species must include complete protection of its habitat.*

We may worry about the future of rare species or rainforests, but few of us know how such issues are tackled legally from one country to another. What is the point, after all, of U.S. law protecting a migratory bird that then reaches its wintering grounds in South America only to be shot? Wildlife protection must be on a worldwide basis to be effective. International environmental law is still a relatively new field, but it is showing how public concern and pressure can shape global legislation.

When countries want to establish international rules for wildlife conservation, they list their obligations in a treaty. These treaties should require their signatories to review implementation regularly and should set up watchdog bodies to check on and assist countries in implementing conservation measures. Participating countries are usually required to make the treaties part of their national law, so that their own authorities can, for example, confiscate illegally traded animals and plants and impose fines for such offenses.

Some wildlife treaties have been drawn up in reaction to the plight of a particular species. A good example of this is the fight to save the vicuña, a South American relative of the llama. This animal was hunted almost to extinction due to world demand for its wool. The La Paz Agreement, signed in 1969 by five South American countries, prohibited killing the vicuña for its meat, skin, or wool. Vicuña populations then recovered to the extent that in 1977 Peru began a culling program, claiming that the numbers had risen to such a level that some animals were starving. Other countries dis-

Right: *Irritated by the IWC bans, which they view as legalistic and outdated, the major whaling nations frequently breach international law.*

Below: *Despite international protection, the walrus is still killed for its magnificent ivory tusks, which can reach about three feet in length.*

puted the need for a cull, however. Eventually, the 1979 Lima Convention was drawn up to allow limited culling. The two vicuña agreements not only banned hunting and international trade, but they also required signatories to conserve the animal's habitat. Most important, the treaties led to the creation of an international body to oversee vicuña conservation.

International law has also had some success in halting the slaughter of whales, most of which inhabit open sea beyond national boundaries. The International Convention for the Regulation of Whaling went into effect in 1948. The treaty established the International Whaling Commission (IWC), which meets annually to adopt regulations on the numbers of whales that can be caught and which species can be hunted.

In its early days the IWC was simply trying to help whale stocks recover so that killing could begin again, as before. Faced with dwindling stocks and growing public pressure, however, the IWC was forced to become more conservationist in approach.

The need for conservation became so critical that in 1982 the IWC prohibited any commercial whaling during the 1985–86 hunting season until further notice. The three main whaling states—Japan, Norway, and the former Soviet Union—objected to this, and whaling continued until 1988. The ban has therefore been in place for just over four years. But even during this period several countries have abused a provision in the treaty that permits whaling for scientific purposes. This loophole means that whale products can still be bought.

At the 43rd meeting of the IWC in 1991, the whaling nations attempted to overturn the ban on commercial whaling. The following year Iceland formally left the IWC and founded its own whaling organization. The hunting of whales is still a contentious issue, but among most participating coun-

on International Trade in Endangered Species (CITES), which originally focused on identifying and stopping the trade in endangered species. This was signed in 1975, and 133 states are now party to it.

It is easy to see the problems involved in implementing international wildlife law in a case like the CITES ban on the ivory trade. The African elephant was given Appendix I (maximum) protection by CITES in 1989, ending the trade in ivory that had put the species' survival at risk. At the annual conference of parties to CITES in March 1992, five African states requested that restricted trade be allowed to resume. They argue that there must be some trade to make it worthwhile—and economically possible—for their people to conserve the elephant.

Other states are against this, saying that resuming any sort of trade opens up the market to poachers as well as legitimate traders. But those states which endorse the ban must be prepared to send money both for conservation programs and to compensate African countries for lost trade. Otherwise, these countries are likely to pull out

tries, it seems that the original objective of the IWC treaty—to allow continued exploitation—is giving way to an ideal that is more sympathetic toward whales.

One of the more successful treaties for wildlife protection has been the Convention

Left: *The 1979 Lima Convention safeguards the vicuña's habitat in the high-altitude grasslands of the Andes.*

Right: *Protective legislation arrived none too soon for the snow leopard and its coveted coat. This cat lives in remote regions where it is very difficult to control poaching.*

of the treaty—leaving no protection for the African elephant.

Wildlife treaties do not just aid specific species; they also seek to protect habitats. The international treaty for the protection of European habitats is the Convention on the Conservation of European Wildlife and Natural Habitats—known as the Berne Convention—which took effect in 1982. Signatories to this treaty undertake to conserve wildlife and wildlife habitats in general and to provide special protection for species. Countries signing the treaty must also take measures to maintain populations of all animal and plant species at levels that correspond to ecological, scientific, and cultural requirements—even if this means sacrificing economic interests. The treaty provides for an all-important watchdog organization, regular meetings of the parties, and reporting requirements.

Nongovernmental organizations (NGOs) have a key role both in developing international environmental legislation and in ensuring its enforcement. Environmental NGOs are not recognized in international law—they cannot take a country to court—but they do attend conferences involving both the negotiation and drafting of treaties. The World Conservation Union (IUCN), for example, played a major role in the initiation and drafting of CITES, and Greenpeace

International has been involved in the negotiation of virtually all international environmental treaties in the past decade. There is little doubt that without the intervention of NGOs, the decision to promote the African elephant to CITES Appendix I would not have taken place.

The role of the NGOs has shown that ordinary people can have a say in the making of environmental law. You can help in your own area by helping to protect any species listed as threatened or endangered. Keep an eye out for these species and bring any abuse to the attention of organizations like the National Wildlife Federation, Sierra Club, or the National Audubon Society. Make sure that traders in wildlife have no one to sell to—do not buy ivory or exotic birds, for example. Another very positive thing you can do is to support groups like the ones just mentioned, as well as World Wildlife Fund, Friends of the Earth, and Greenpeace. They really do help in the legal protection of the world's wildlife.

Despite the great concern that many people feel for the future of the species sharing the planet with us, there is currently no worldwide treaty for the protection of habitats or ecosystems at risk. The 1992 Earth Summit in Rio proved that the economic interests of developed nations continue to override the need for conservation measures to safeguard wildlife for the future. Without the will of individual countries, international law alone cannot hope to provide the way.

Helen Clapperton

Above: *Ironically, some conservationists are among the loudest voices calling for a resumption in ivory trading. The ivory ban, they contend, leaves Africans with no financial motive for protecting the elephant.*

Left: *The deforestation of Indonesian islands is largely to blame for the babirusa's decline, despite its listing in CITES Appendix I.*

145

TEAMING UP TO SAVE THE ENVIRONMENT

Above: *In the Pacific Northwest, the National Wildlife Federation is trying to save the salmon population. Dams on the Columbia and Snake rivers are obstacles to adult fish migrating to their spawning grounds and young traveling downriver to the sea.*

Right: *Youngsters at NWF's Wildlife Camp learn firsthand about life in a stream. "Wildlife Camp isn't like any other camp," explains Susan Johnson, manager of the NWF Youth Programs. "It is a carefully planned outdoor experience designed to develop the love of nature."*

"We're all in this together!" With this statement, the National Wildlife Federation (NWF) recently brought the plight of endangered species to the attention of children in over 620,000 classrooms as part of its annual National Wildlife Week. Colorful posters depicting animals and plants in trouble—from the aye-aye through the gavial and the pitcher plant to the zebra—underlined the importance of all living things on this planet. A variety of suggested activities encouraged children to find out about their endangered environment and join in the effort to save it.

The assertion "We're all in this together!" echoes throughout NWF's programs. This organization reaches out to people of all ages, from preschoolers on up, to let them know about environmental problems and to help them take action to protect both wildlife and habitats. Underlying these efforts is a belief that by joining with other environmentally concerned citizens in an organized campaign, each person can truly make a difference.

The call for a unified attack in the fight to safeguard the environment was initially made in the mid-1930s by Jay N. "Ding" Darling, a prominent conservationist and political cartoonist. Angry at Congress' lack of action on environmental issues, he persuaded President Franklin D. Roosevelt to convene the first North American Wildlife Conference. At this meeting representatives of farmers, hunters, women's groups, gardening clubs, Boy Scouts, and Girl Scouts decided to increase their political clout by banding together in an umbrella organization called the General Wildlife Federation,

which was later renamed the National Wildlife Federation.

Since that time NWF has grown into one of the largest conservation organizations in the United States, with more than five million members. In addition to its headquarters in Washington, D.C., NWF operates an educational center in Virginia and natural resource centers in eight different regions of the United States. Its network includes affiliate organizations in 49 states and the Virgin Islands.

Educating children, teenagers, and adults about environmental issues is a major focus of the National Wildlife Federation. Preschoolers are invited to explore the world of plants and animals through full-page photographs, simple puzzles, and read-to-me stories in the monthly magazine *Your Big Backyard.* School-age children enjoy learning about creatures as different as ibexes, giraffe weevils, rubber boas, and California condors in another monthly publication, *Ranger Rick.* In every issue a story about Ranger Rick (a raccoon character) highlights a conservation problem, such as damage by tourists in Yellowstone, and lets children know what they can do about it.

To help schoolteachers bring environmental issues and science to life in the classroom, NWF has devised the *NatureScope* series, containing background information, hands-on learning projects, worksheets, and puzzles. Each "kit" investigates a specific topic, such as insects, dinosaurs, geology, or rainforests. There is also a video that shows what students in different parts of the United States are doing to help save the Earth.

Above: *The National Wildlife Federation is monitoring the red-cockaded woodpecker population, which is affected by clearcutting in old pine forests in the Southeast. The red feathers that give this woodpecker its name are usually covered by its black crown feathers.*

During the summer NWF runs several camps where youngsters can have fun and explore nature at the same time. Campers learn how to "read" animal tracks, identify different species, make natural dyes from plants, and use camping techniques that help preserve the environment. Teenagers have a chance to go backpacking for 12 days in wilderness areas in the Blue Ridge mountains in North Carolina or in the Colorado Rockies.

For entire families, as well as couples and single adults, NWF holds Conservation Summits—week-long outdoor discovery programs in scenic locations such as California's Monterey Peninsula or Big Sky, Montana. There are field trips and classes on a range of topics from ecology to nature photography, as well as special activities for children. Teachers can participate in a special Educators' Summit in order to find out how to weave environmental concerns into the curriculum.

To keep its adult members informed on conservation issues, NWF puts out *National Wildlife* and *International Wildlife.* These bimonthly magazines feature instructive articles by naturalists and vivid photographs, as well as updates on pressing environmental problems, with information on what individuals can do. For members who want to take an active role in influencing federal and state legislation, NWF sends out *Enviroaction,* a news digest, as well as regular "Action Alerts" with information on where to write to make a difference.

NWF doesn't stop at teaching the public about conservation; it also actively educates the government. Working together with other environmental groups, it directly pressures Congress to pass laws to protect endangered species, preserve wildlife habitats, regulate hazardous wastes, control water pollution, and the like. When abuses of existing laws occur, NWF lawyers are ready to fight these violations in court.

Right: *NWF's Alaska Center is focusing on wetlands protection. The Copper River Delta as well as other wetlands in Alaska provide breeding grounds for more than 80 percent of the world's trumpeter swans. Once endangered, this swan has made a comeback but could be threatened again if its Alaska habitat is destroyed.*

Staff members at the NWF Natural Resource Centers passionately describe a host of problems the National Wildlife Federation is currently tackling. In the Florida Keys, for example, NWF is fighting in the courts to prevent development, which threatens the tiny Key deer, an endangered species. "Each year," David White explains, "more deer are killed than are born. Most are hit by cars." NWF recently helped stop Monroe County from constructing a new road that would have let 3,500 cars a day travel through Key deer habitat. It is now suing the Federal Emergency Management Agency, which refuses to acknowledge it has any responsibility to endangered species and continues to provide low-cost flood insurance to developers in the Keys.

The Southeastern Center is also keeping a close eye on the red-cockaded woodpecker, an unusual bird that excavates cavities only in living trees 70 to 90 years old. Like the northern spotted owl, this bird is threatened by clearcutting in old forests. The red-cockaded woodpecker is considered an indicator species—a drop in its population indicates that its habitat and other species in that habitat are in danger.

In the Midwest NWF is battling to improve water quality in the Great Lakes. "Despite progress in the last 20 years," says Mark Van Putten, "polluters are still legally dumping PCBs, dioxin, mercury, and other chemicals into the Great Lakes . . . poisons making fish unsafe to eat and causing death and birth defects in wildlife." People— especially children—who eat fish from the Great Lakes are at risk for health problems.

One Great Lake—Lake Superior—still has relatively high-quality water. As Tim Eder and Gayle Coyer both underline, the challenge is to preserve this lake *before* it becomes polluted. Although the U.S. and Canadian governments have pledged to limit pollution and eventually make the lake

a zero-discharge zone, this is a pledge on paper. NWF is suing major polluters like the Copper Range Company to ensure that the lake stays clean.

Throughout the United States NWF is fighting to protect wetlands—a critical habitat for 43 percent of the threatened or endangered species in the country. A recent NWF report reveals that the nation's wetlands "are being destroyed at the dizzying rate of 35 acres an hour." In the prairie states, Skip Baron reports, NWF is on the alert for any farmers who try to alter wetlands in order to plant crops. At the same time it is working to replenish lost wetlands.

Above: *If Lake Superior is to stay relatively clean, it needs to be protected now. NWF is working with the Lake Superior Alliance, a coalition of national and grass-roots groups, to preserve the lake's ecosystem.*

In cooperation with state and federal agencies, other environmental groups, and corporations, NWF has helped raise money to purchase and restore drained wetlands in South Dakota—benefiting pintails, mallards, blue-winged teal, and other animals.

The battle to preserve existing wetlands is particularly urgent in Alaska, according to Ann Rothe. Almost 70 percent of the nation's wetlands are in Alaska, but thousands of acres may be destroyed if oil companies get their way and developers are exempted from the government regulations that protect wetlands in other states. Over 70,000 swans, a million geese, and 12 million ducks depend on Alaska's wetlands. Hundreds of millions of shorebirds use these wetlands, and 96 percent of all U.S. seabirds rely on them directly or indirectly. Alaska's wetlands are also critical for five species of Pacific salmon. By acting now,

Rothe points out, it may be possible to avoid the dire situation in the Pacific Northwest, where all major salmon runs are endangered or threatened.

The Pacific Northwest Center—which has already helped win the first round in the struggle to protect old-growth forests from the logging industry and save species like the northern spotted owl—is now making every effort to save the salmon population. "The resource that symbolizes the Pacific Northwest is about to collapse," warns Jacqui Bonomo. Already the sockeye salmon that gave Idaho's Redfish Lake its name has virtually disappeared, and 179 salmon stocks are at risk. NWF is pressuring the Northwest Power Planning Council to ensure that fish and wildlife get equal protection with industries that utilize western rivers.

At the Rocky Mountain Center, Tom

Below: The National Wildlife Federation is fighting to save Florida's 250 or so remaining Key deer. This white-tailed deer, which is only about the size of a large dog, has already lost much of its habitat to resort development. Speeding cars are now the Key deer's major enemy.

Left: *The ocelot is one of twelve endangered species featured in NWF's Educator's Kit for 1992 Wildlife Week, which had the theme "We're all in this together." This dark-spotted cat is still illegally hunted for the fur trade in Latin America. In the United States only 80 to 120 animals remain in secluded areas in Texas and Arizona.*

Dougherty stresses, grazing reform is a central issue. Approximately 80 percent of all wildlife species in the West live near rivers or streams, yet these areas are being trampled and "cleared" by cattle at the public's expense. As a recent NWF report notes, the federal government spends $50 million a year to subsidize grazing on public lands in a program that benefits a number of rich livestock owners. Ranchers pay less than $2 a head to graze their animals on federal land, when the going rate on private land is about $9 a head. Most grazing decisions are open to public review, however, so citizens can have an impact. Any local citizen can become an "affected interest" with regard to a particular parcel of government land, explains Dougherty. The government then has to inform that citizen of any grazing decisions affecting that land, and the citizen has the right to complain. NWF and its affiliates are busy organizing citizens to do just that.

The National Wildlife Federation is involved in many other projects, including the highly successful Backyard Wildlife Habitat Program, which helps people turn their gardens into wildlife habitats. At every level there's the sense that preserving our environment is a team effort, bringing numerous individuals together. Just how effective a team approach is can be seen in NWF's campus outreach program, Cool It! Students have joined up with faculty and administrators to develop recycling programs, conduct energy audits, and implement tree-planting projects. A number of colleges have even organized "Green Cup" championships, with dorms competing to see which one can save the most energy. In its first year at Harvard, this contest saved the university $100,000, according to Nick Keller. Multiply savings like that across campus after campus, and you will understand just how much impact grassroots efforts can have. Remember: "We're all in this together!"

Sue Heinemann

RAINBOW WARRIORS

Above: *Greenpeace protesters board a Polaris submarine at the Faslane base near Glasgow to draw attention to its cracked nuclear reactor.*

Right: *The new Rainbow Warrior was launched four years after the bombing of its predecessor.*

Below. *The Greenpeace base in Antarctica (now dismantled) played a vital role in the fight to preserve the continent.*

Under a threateningly gray sky, a buzzing swarm of inflatable rafts speed over the choppy sea, their yellow radiation warning flags flapping bravely in the breeze. As the first Polaris submarine looms into view, the tension in the rafts becomes almost palpable as the crews prepare themselves for the confrontation ahead.

In perfect unison the rafts break ranks and begin darting around the docks while navy-clad sailors look on. Suddenly, one of the rafts heads straight toward the smooth flank of a sub. As the small craft lunges onto the berthed hulk, two of the crew members leap aboard and unfurl a black-and-white banner. The image is stark and needs no explanation. As the banner's ragged white line splits the expanse of black steel, its graphic depiction of the cracked nuclear reactor in this submarine is clear for all the world's media to see.

Within minutes the coup is complete. But the message endures. Once again a threat to the environment has been confronted directly, confronted by arguably the most dynamic of all the environmental pressure groups: Greenpeace.

Whether driving their tiny boats between a great whale and the explosive harpoon of a Japanese whaler or blocking the polluting discharge of a factory outfall pipe, there is no mistaking the Greenpeace style. It is bold. It is confrontational. And it is effective.

Greenpeace has been pursuing its campaign of nonviolent direct action ever since 1971, when a group of North American activists sailed the *Phyllis Cormack* into the U.S. atomic test zone off Amchitka, Alaska, to protest against the continued testing of nuclear weapons.

From that characteristically bold beginning, Greenpeace has grown into one of the most potent pressure groups, with over five million supporters drawn from nearly 160 different countries. Yet despite the administrative problems that could accompany such growth, Greenpeace has lost none of its radical cutting edge. It has preserved this partly by keeping its aims simple and partly by maintaining a very streamlined chain of command.

Today, Greenpeace operates on the same basic premise that it adopted 21 years ago: that determined individuals can alter the actions and purposes of even the overwhelmingly powerful by bearing witness —that is, by drawing attention to an environmental abuse through their unwavering presence, whatever the risk. And by bearing witness, Greenpeace can not only inform the public of this crime against the environment, but can also—if only temporarily—stop the crime itself.

While Greenpeace has remained true to its founding principle, the world it seeks to protect has changed immensely. During the 1970s and early 1980s, environmental issues were of minor interest. Today, however, they command far more attention. And while this trend is to be welcomed, it

Above: *British chemical giant ICI produced over 22,000 tons of ozone-destroying chemicals in 1990, about a quarter of which were CFCs. Despite agreeing to stop producing some CFCs in 1993, ICI intends to import the very same chemicals from the Netherlands.*

brings with it new responsibilities for environmental pressure groups.

This point is not lost on Peter Melchett, the executive director of Greenpeace UK: "Today there are far more journalists and people in government who understand the issues. So in one sense at least the political climate is far tougher now for groups such as Greenpeace. We must be much more professional; we must do more research and take more expert scientific advice, for we know that our arguments will have to stand close scrutiny."

As well as being scientifically sound, it is also important that Greenpeace get its message across in a clear and consistent manner. It achieves this by having a surprisingly centralized management structure. All its major campaigns are selected by Greenpeace International, which is run by a five-person board elected by representatives from the 30 or so national offices. The cam-

paigns of Greenpeace USA, like those run by other national offices, are then taken from this campaign list, the choice being based on the appropriateness of the campaign to the country concerned and the availability of suitable resources.

As an entirely independent organization, Greenpeace's resources are derived almost entirely from its supporters. After years of steady growth, Greenpeace saw an explosive surge in support during 1985 following the bombing of the *Rainbow Warrior* in Aukland, New Zealand, by the French Secret Service, and the trend continued the following year after the Chernobyl disaster. But the main growth in support occurred between 1987 and 1990, as environmental issues increasingly stole the political limelight. By 1992 Greenpeace USA had around 1.7 million supporters.

Greenpeace began its campaigning at sea, and it still remains closely identified with the protection of the marine environment. But today the issues it tackles are far more wide-ranging. In 1992 the key campaigns run from the U.S. office included atmosphere and energy concerns (for example, ozone depletion), toxics, civilian and military nuclear issues, ocean ecology, and tropical and domestic forests.

"Atmosphere and energy" is the newest of the Greenpeace campaigns. As campaigner Charlie Kronick explains, "It grew out of the campaign against acid rain, which was originally aimed chiefly at reducing the emissions from power stations. But as global warming became an issue our dependence on fossil fuels—and in particular their consumption by cars—had to be addressed.

"Cars already produce 15 percent of global CO_2, yet the world's car population of half a billion is set to double in 20 years. As a result of this growth, the CO_2 emissions in Britain from cars alone would exceed the limits agreed on by the British government

even if they shut down every coal-fired power station in the country."

As part of its atmosphere and energy campaign, Greenpeace has carried out many direct actions: from hanging banners from giant smokestacks to dangling a massive plug from a hot-air balloon over the sulfurous chimneys of a power station in Yorkshire, England. But in some cases—such as the campaign to save sea turtles—direct action is simply not appropriate.

Based in the U.K. offices, Catherine Barr of Greenpeace International has been working on this campaign for the past two years. There are seven species of sea turtle and all are currently endangered. Despite this, large numbers are still being killed for their shells and meat.

With its special interest in ocean ecology, Greenpeace was the obvious group to try to relieve the turtles' desperate plight. But as Catherine points out, "Knowing that the turtles were in trouble was just the start; the

You'll need more than a brave face when the ozone goes

Soon we could all be wearing brightly coloured sun-block. Why? Because government scientists warn that some chemicals produced by industry are destroying the ozone layer (the earth's own protective sun-screen) over Britain. This means more harmful radiation from the sun will get through to us. And, if we don't take care, this could damage our eyes and cause skin cancers. Children are especially at risk.

GREENPEACE

Above: *Following the revelation by NASA scientists that an ozone hole over the Northern Hemisphere could be imminent, Greenpeace stepped up its campaign to publicize the risks to health should this protective layer be destroyed by man-made chemicals such as CFCs.*

Left: *To commemorate the fifth anniversary of the Chernobyl disaster, Greenpeace planted 5,000 crosses outside the Soviet-built Bohunice nuclear power plant in Czechoslovakia, as part of its campaign to put pressure on the Czech government to shut this plant down.*

Right: *Despite being listed on Appendix I of the Convention on International Trade in Endangered Species, sea turtles are still being slaughtered.*

Overleaf: *Preserving Antarctica is regarded as one of Greenpeace's greatest triumphs.*

Far right: *The use of automobiles is the most polluting activity on earth. With a new car produced each second, the number of cars is growing faster than the human population.*

Below: *Greenpeace campaigners on Sugar Loaf Mountain express their feelings about the Rio Conference. Their banner dwarfs that of fellow protesters from Climb for the Earth.*

next step was to identify which areas of the world needed most attention.

"Japan proved to be the main market driving the trade, and Indonesia the country where more sea turtles are taken than anywhere else, with around 70,000 green and hawksbill turtles being killed every year."

With no Indonesian office, it was vital for the Greenpeace International campaigners to adopt a soft-sell approach and to work closely with the local people and conservation groups. "One of the first tasks facing us was to learn how Balinese law works," explains Catherine.

"It was also crucial for us to explain who we were and why we wanted to protect the turtles. This we achieved in part through a carefully translated letter to the governor of Bali explaining that turtles are migratory and may nest as far away as Australia. We pointed out that they were killing animals which are, in effect, international."

The main thrust of the campaign that followed was aimed at tourists going to Bali. Tour operators, airlines, travel agents, hotels, and the media were all informed of the turtles' plight and urged to support a ban on the trade in sea turtle products.

This measured approach paid off. After further meetings with the governor, legislation was drafted that will ban the killing of hawksbill turtles in Indonesia. Proposals have also been put forward to reduce the number of green turtles killed from 20,000 to 3,000 over the next few years.

Species-specific campaigns are useful as a focus, but it is dangerous to view them in isolation, as everything in the real world is linked. Campaigns to protect the seas or the rainforests not only make more sense from an ecological point of view, but they also allow Greenpeace to maximize its resources. No one appreciates this better than Peter Melchett, who comments: "In the future we will probably do fewer campaigns but put more resources into them. We will also strive to set clearer goals and present clearer messages, because at the end of the day, we survive on public support. We have to do and say things that mean something to people of many different countries and cultures. Politicians don't listen to what we say because it's clever, or because we have a fleet of ships, but because we have five million supporters."

Despite their diversity, Greenpeace supporters can be broadly characterized: most are under 40 years old and display a more passionate commitment to Greenpeace itself than is typical of the supporters of many other pressure groups. This fervor perhaps

reflects the tremendous strength of spirit possessed by the organization itself. For despite the depressing nature of the many challenges faced by Greenpeace, the optimism and commitment within the organization is overwhelming—and contagious. As Peter Melchett says, "I am only interested in winning campaigns. And although it has been suggested that as we have grown bigger we have become less radical, less effective—the reality is that today Greenpeace

does far more direct actions, on far more issues, in far more countries against far more powerful opponents that we ever did in the early days."

In 1992, after 21 years of campaigning, Greenpeace scored a particularly symbolic victory. In the spirit of the crew of the *Phyllis Cormack*, which challenged the American nuclear test program in the North Pacific, Greenpeace campaigners aboard the new *Rainbow Warrior* confronted the French in the South Pacific. As a result of this brave, defiant nonviolent action, the French government was finally persuaded to introduce a moratorium on nuclear weapons testing, bringing us all one step closer to a green and peaceful world.

John Birdsall

NOT ALL DOOM AND GLOOM

Greenpeace has focused world attention on many of the most shocking environmental atrocities, and not surprisingly, the green message frequently appears to be a depressingly dark one. But throughout its 21-year history, Greenpeace has won an impressive number of victories, and it is upon these past successes that hope for the future rests.

• Following a protest at the test site at Amchitka, Alaska, in 1972, the U.S. nuclear testing program was abandoned after one explosion.

• A worldwide campaign that drew attention to the brutal slaughter of seal pups for their skins led in 1982 to a European Community (EC) ban on the import of seal skins.

• Intensive lobbying proved instrumental in the 1983 ban on the dumping of radioactive waste at sea.

• The "Save the Whale" campaign finally achieved a major success when the International Whaling Commission banned commercial whaling in 1986.

• After a campaign against the incineration of toxic wastes at sea, a worldwide ban was enacted in 1988.

• In 1990 the North Sea Ministers Conference endorsed a wide range of measures to clean up the North Sea. The British government also agreed to end waste dumping by 1993 and sewage dumping by 1998.

• In 1991, after lobbying by the Antarctic Treaty nations, a 50-year ban on mineral extraction in Antarctica was passed.

• After a six-year campaign, Japan announced that by the end of 1992 it would stop large-scale drift netting. The EC also announced a similar ban.

THE COMMUNICATORS & EDUCATORS

It is easy to take our interest in and knowledge of the world's animals for granted. Yet it was not so long ago that people viewed the great outdoors and its inhabitants with indifference or even hostility. It took visionary and courageous individuals to move the study of wildlife away from the cramped confines of zoos and museums out into natural habitats. Just as important, their skill in communicating their findings captured the public imagination and turned many of us into amateur natural historians.

Today, the descendants of these first popular naturalists continue to spread the wildlife word. We look at the work of wildlife sound recordist Jeremy West and talk with popular author Gerald Durrell. Next we salute the pioneers of natural history and then go behind the scenes with researchers who are working on behalf of Florida's endangered manatees.

Finally, we conclude with a profile of Richard Barnwell, who worked as a game warden in Nigeria for nine years. His story is one of a truly hands-on experience with wildlife.

Left: Recent research on bears has shed new light on these much-maligned loners.

Below: Gerald Durrell's books have brought the world of nature to people worldwide.

Left: Wildlife tourism is becoming increasingly popular. But only a few people are lucky enough to study wildlife in the field, and even fewer get to make it their career.

BEHIND THE MICROPHONE OF A
WILDLIFE SOUND RECORDIST

Above: *For Jeremy West, sound is like a colorful brushstroke that enriches and brings life to his perception of the environment.*

Right: *Stealthy recording in the reed beds of Botswana in Africa rewarded Jeremy with the unforgettable sound of frolicking hippos.*

One of the great things about wildlife sound recording is that it requires only a small investment in equipment. At a minimum you need a portable tape recorder, a parabolic reflector, a microphone, and a set of headphones—and that is just how I started. I have always enjoyed traveling in remote places in all parts of the world and had planned an overland drive to Spain, to go walking in the Sierra Nevada. I took a portable cassette recorder quite by chance and was fascinated by the sounds I heard along the way—cuckoos, nightingales, a plowman's commands to his mule, donkeys braying, goats' bells, and the richly varied sounds of mountain streams. The quality of these first recordings left a lot to be desired, but it did inspire me to learn more. I got advice from Richard Margoschis of the Wildlife Sound Recording Society (WSRS) during one of his weekend courses on recording wildlife sounds. I upgraded from cassette to quarter-inch tape, bought some second-hand equipment, and built a four-track studio in my London home—all at surprisingly little expense.

Then the adventure began. For the first two years, I recorded anything I could, from wildlife to music, speech to machinery, raindrops to crackling campfires. All the time I was discussing my recordings with anyone even remotely involved in sound in order to find the best ways to sell my material. I knew I wanted to take sound recording seriously and go professional.

Today I make the main part of my living by recording soundtrack for film, especially for adventure documentaries. One expedition took me to the coast of northern Chile,

AN INTERVIEW WITH
GERALD DURRELL

Above: *"I get floods of people saying what an influence reading my books has been on them. It's very flattering, and if it's true, it's what I always wanted to do with my life."*

Right: *The black-and-white ruffed lemur, threatened by habitat destruction in its native Madagascar, is one of many species that are bred in Jersey.*

Let's make one thing clear, right away, for those who haven't read Gerald Durrell's popular books on animals. The man doesn't just like animals, he loves them. And he is quite unashamed to admit it.

"Every time I see an animal I think, now that's the animal for me! If I see a giraffe, I say, 'How marvelous, how wonderful, seeing that lovely female giraffe, I wish I were a male giraffe. That long neck, those long legs, just like an American film star.'

"Then I see a babirusa [a wild pig from Indonesia with an impressive set of tusks], and I think, 'Isn't that absolutely the most marvelous thing in the world!' Though I admit I wouldn't want to kiss one. Then I see a chimpanzee or a gorilla; and there's my wife—she's a primate too, you know."

Some zoo directors or conservationists may find this attitude embarrassingly un-scientific. But the founder and honorary director of the Jersey Wildlife Preservation Trust, on the island of Jersey in the English Channel, is not your average zoo director or conservationist. Nor does he claim any great scientific knowledge. "My wife, Lee, is more scientifically qualified than I am," he claims. "I am the most ignorant man I know. But my talent is knowing how to put things together and getting other people to do them . . . and getting all the credit!"

Gerry wanted his own zoo from the age of six or so, an ambition that grew and grew, to the consternation of friends and relatives. His first trip, to Cameroon in 1950, resulted in a collection of 500 creatures, which he sold to two zoos. He immortalized the trip in *The Overloaded Ark*, the first of many de-lightful best-sellers about animals.

Right: *Alfred Russel Wallace contributed to the theory of evolution. Although he developed his theory of natural selection independently of Charles Darwin, be was quite generous in sharing his findings with the other great British naturalist.*

Walter Bates (1825–1892), and Alfred Russel Wallace (1823–1913). All traveled for long periods in South America, and each later achieved a reputation as a distinguished field naturalist. The first of these, however, went further, for Darwin is undoubtedly the single most important naturalist of the 19th century. His book *The Origin of Species* described the mechanism regulating the living world—the process that we know as natural selection. The image we have inherited of this great scientist is of a heavy-browed, white-bearded sage. Yet in early manhood Darwin was also an adventurous traveler, spending six years on board HMS *Beagle*, which took him to the Cape Verde islands, the Galápagos Islands, Tahiti, New Zealand, and Tasmania.

Darwin's account of this journey, *Journal of Researches into the Geology and Natural History of the Various Countries Visited*

Right: John James Audubon's illustrations —like this trio of ivory-billed woodpeckers— are remarkable both for their painstaking detail and the vivid way they conjure up a bird's movement.

rejected these methods. None of his publications better demonstrates his approach than his immensely popular *Wanderings in South America.*

Published in 1825, the book is an account of his Amazonian journeys, full of exotic tales of his encounters with the natural world. Waterton recalled, for instance, how he had left his toes protruding from his camp bed as a lure for bloodsucking vampire bats, so that he could observe their feeding behavior at close quarters. He also described an encounter with a large crocodile—a black cayman. He leapt on its back and wrestled with it before his servants finally captured the creature. Accounts like these provoked disbelief among his peers, yet his book fascinated its 19th-century audience, and it encouraged a generation of younger naturalists to follow in his adventurous footsteps.

Three young men who were inspired by works of natural history like Waterton's were Charles Darwin (1809–1882), Henry

during the Voyage by HMS Beagle, was published in 1839. Its lengthy title disguises the most personal and, for the layperson, most enjoyable of Darwin's publications. Like Waterton's *Wanderings in South America*, it presents natural history as an exciting process, not just as a matter of examining dried bones and pickled skins.

Henry Bates and Alfred Wallace were naturalists and authors in exactly the same mold. However, unlike Waterton or Darwin, they did not inherit a private income. They financed their joint expedition to the Amazonian forests by selling the skins that they collected. Setting out in 1848, Bates and Wallace traveled up the Amazon for almost two years. Eventually the two men parted company. Wallace remained in South America another two years, while Bates stayed for nine more years. Bates, a meticulous field naturalist, amassed a huge number of specimens, representing 14,712 species. Of this total, 8,000—most of them insects— were completely new to science. Bates's account of his 11-year expedition, *The Naturalist on the River Amazon*, published in 1863, is a classic work of natural history exploration that remains widely read today.

Although Bates's reputation as an author rests on this one work, Alfred Wallace was a prolific writer on a wide range of subjects. Moreover, his own journeys in tropical regions exceeded the travels of his early companion. After spending four years in South America, Wallace switched his attention to the rainforests of Southeast Asia. There he remained for eight years. As a consequence of his studies, Wallace developed, independently of Darwin, the idea that all life forms had evolved as a result of the process of natural selection. This momentous theory was first announced at a scientific meeting in 1858, in a paper written by both men.

Wallace remained a staunch supporter of Darwin's ideas about the origins of life, and he was one of the most important thinkers on evolution in the 19th century. He also wrote autobiographical works describing his expeditions in the tropics, such as *Travels on the Amazon and Rio Negro* and *The Malay Archipelago*.

However important the scientific papers and books of authors like Wallace, it was not the written word alone that brought the world of nature alive for Victorian society. Improvements in both the quality and the supply of paper, the development of the steam-powered press, and important inno-

Below: *John James Audubon produced illustrations of great accuracy and quality, which left the public clamoring for more.*

Above & right: *"The Ancient Wrasse" is from* **The Aquarium,** *by the Victorian writer and illustrator Philip Henry Gosse. Such works led to a vogue for aquariums.*

Below: *Early naturalists were lampooned by contemporaries as harmless eccentrics, as in this Swedish cartoon of the household of Sir William Buckland.*

vations in color-printing methods paved the way for an array of gifted wildlife artists to help popularize the subject.

Perhaps the most important of these was John James Audubon, an American born in 1785. As a young man, Audubon neglected business and family to devote himself to his wildlife paintings. In 1826 he visited Britain to generate financial support for his legendary book, *The Birds of America.* The completion of this work in 1838 was in every sense a colossal achievement. The four volumes each measured more than three feet high and over two feet wide, and altogether they contained 435 plates. By drawing from freshly killed birds to obtain the truest colors and depicting his specimens life-size or larger, Audubon produced what is probably the most famous collection of bird paintings ever. In 1984 a full set of this magnificent work sold for over $1.5 million.

Audubon's art inspired a wide public demand for large-format collections of animal paintings and created a climate in which younger wildlife artists could flourish. One

such figure was John Gould. Born in 1804, he was the most important British painter of birds in the 19th century, although "publisher" might more accurately describe his own role. The paintings were completed by his wife, Elizabeth, and a team of talented artists including Edward Lear, the writer of nonsense verse. However, it was Gould who had the business acumen to ensure that his many volumes of color plates—including his five-volume *The Birds of Europe*, published between 1832 and 1837, and the subsequent seven-volume *Birds of Australia*—found an enthusiastic audience.

In their efforts to stimulate public interest in wildlife paintings, men like Audubon and Gould had a number of advantages, which related to the qualities of their subjects—the birds themselves. Highly varied, easily visible, dynamic, and often exquisitely beautiful, birds made almost ideal subjects for these artists. Many of the naturalists who were confined to the written word, like Wallace or Bates, also had an advantage in capturing their audience's imagination—the inherent drama of exotic locations. No such advantages, however, were available to Phillip Henry Gosse. For Gosse, who was born in 1810, concentrated primarily on marine biology. Many of his animal subjects were visible only with the aid of a microscope.

This might seem unpromising territory for a best-seller, yet Gosse became one of the most popular authors writing on natural history in the mid-Victorian period. While his early works—*The Canadian Naturalist* and *Birds of Jamaica*—focused on the wildlife he had seen during his 12 years in the Americas, Gosse's most successful books had titles such as *The Ocean, A Naturalist's Rambles on the Devonshire Coast, Seaside Pleasures, The Aquarium,* and *Evenings at the Microscope.* In addition to showing considerable talents as an illustrator and writer, Gosse was one of the first to discover that aquatic life, from sea anemones to prawns or fish, could be maintained and studied in the home when kept in a glass case. Thanks to his book *A Naturalist's Rambles on the Devonshire Coast,* aquariums became fashionable additions to the drawing rooms of thousands of Victorian homes.

In books such as *The Aquarium,* Gosse used the latest techniques of chromolithography and was one of the first to include color plates in a work directed at a mass market. Through his exploration of this new technology, Gosse alerted his Victorian audience to the strange and often beautiful creatures that existed inside a seaside rock pool. His innovation demonstrates a quality that unites all these gifted and extraordinary pioneers. Their efforts awakened an awareness and an understanding of parts of the natural world that had previously been unknown or overlooked. Through their work, they bequeathed a legacy fundamental to our understanding of the world around us.

Mark Cocker

CHARLES DARWIN

As a child and young man, Charles Darwin showed little indication of his future gifts as a scientist. He was unremarkable at school, unmotivated as a medical student at Edinburgh University, and a failure as a trainee clergyman at Cambridge. While he was studying

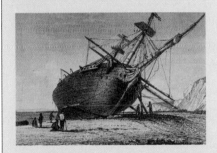

at Cambridge, however, Darwin became an avid collector of beetles, and this hobby led to him being invited to travel as a naturalist on board the HMS Beagle *in 1831.*

It was on this five-year voyage that Darwin discovered his vocation as a naturalist. His detailed observations of wildlife formed the basis of much of his life's work. Near the journey's end, the variations of species he saw on the Galápagos Islands galvanized the insights he had been developing about the evolution of species.

Back in England, however, it was many years before Darwin published his theory of natural selection. In fact it was only in 1858, when Alfred Rus-

sel Wallace was on the verge of publishing his own findings on the same subject, that Darwin was persuaded to present his principles of natural selection to the public. The Origin of Species *caused as much controversy as Darwin had feared. By the time he died in 1882, however, survival of the fittest was a widely accepted premise for life on earth, and the eminent scientist was honored by being buried in Westminster Abbey in London.*

MONITORING
MANATEES

Above: *Manatees use their flexible front flippers for many purposes, including scratching and feeding. Here a manatee cleans its mouth with a rag held in its flippers.*

At the flash of a hand signal in the water, Stormy, a 1,200-pound, seven-year-old manatee, swam to place his head in the wire hoop suspended in his tank. Seconds later, a light came on at the end of the tank, signaling that it was time to swim out of the hoop and bump his lips against a paddle suspended to the right of the light. When he responded correctly, his trainer blew a whistle that told him to collect his reward, a monkey biscuit.

The behavior Stormy was learning will soon be used to develop a manatee hearing test. Stormy will swim to insert his head in the hoop, and a tone will be sounded in the water. When the light comes on, Stormy will indicate if he heard the tone by swimming to the left paddle if he did and to the right if he did not.

In February '92, Dr. Edmund Gerstein of Florida Atlantic University began Stormy's training at Lowry Park Zoo in Tampa. When Dr. Gerstein advances to the hearing test, he will be studying Stormy and another manatee, Dundee, to try to find out why nearly every manatee spotted in Florida's waters seems to have collided with a boat. Could it be that manatees cannot hear approaching boats so they are unable to swim out of harm's way?

The research is part of an effort to protect manatees, seal-like marine mammals sometimes called sea cows, that grow up to 13 feet long and weigh up to 1,500 pounds. Although they have been on the endangered species list for nearly two decades, protection programs have been slow to develop. Under a recovery plan for manatees that got under way in 1983, federal and

Right: *Manatees often gather in small groups to engage in playful activities, which include kissing and embracing. "Play groups" may be made up of adults as well as juveniles.*

Right: *Motorboats pose a serious threat to Florida's manatees, many of which have been killed or injured by the propellers.*

Below: *A female manatee generally gives birth to one calf, but occasionally she may have two. The young suckle for several years, even though they can eat vegetation at about one month old.*

make decisions on which areas are essential to the manatees.

The service is also keeping track of 900 manatees that can be identified by the distinctive scar patterns that are left from their collisions with boats. Each winter, when the manatees congregate at warm-water sources, biologists identify individuals, take photographs, and try to determine the condition and reproductive status of each of the animals. The information is used to gauge birth and death rates and migration patterns.

The injured manatees at the Lowry Park Zoo were being cared for under the recovery plan's mandate to rescue and rehabilitate as many injured or diseased manatees as possible. Rescue teams transport injured animals to one of five ocean areas, such as the Miami Seaquarium, where marine-mammal veterinarians try to nurse them back to health.

"Our goal is to release as many of those animals back into the wild as we can so they can reproduce naturally," said Robert Turner, the manatee-recovery coordinator for the Fish and Wildlife Service. In May 1992, three manatees were released at the Merritt Island National Wildlife Refuge, including a female who had been injured and her calf, which was born in captivity. Most released manatees are fitted with transmitter harnesses so their progress can be tracked.

Although the survival rate for released manatees is good, Mr. Turner said, orphaned calves and rehabilitated manatees that have spent long periods of time in captivity may not know where to go or how to get food. "It's like taking a pet and throwing it into the woods," he explained. In order to improve survival rates for such animals, the service plans to build a special pen at the refuge, sort of a halfway house, where manatees that are ready for release can become acquainted with wild manatees across the fence until they are ready to be turned loose.

The most controversial aspect of the manatee program is the attempt to slow boats down near manatee habitats. The Department of Natural Resources has set speed limits for hundreds of miles of waterways in nine counties and plans new speed limits for four more. The regulations, which are imposed after consultations with the counties, require boats to go very slowly in some manatee gathering spots and travel corridors, and they prohibit all human activities in some areas.

While manatee advocates endorse the plan, many water-skiers and boaters have fought the rules. In Sarasota County, speed zones were adopted in December 1991, and signs were posted in the waterways in July '92. But even before the signs were posted, the County Commission had decided to review the regulations.

Rick Rawlins, owner of the Highland Park Fish Camp in Volusia County, said the rules adopted there last year would put him out of business because the slow-speed zones lengthened the time it took to reach fishing spots.

"The rules would add as much as five to six hours to a day of fishing," Mr. Rawlins said. "My customers are leaving me. Some said they are not going to fish anymore. Others are going to other counties."

Mr. Rawlins has formed a group called Citizens for Responsible Boating to fight the regulations. The group filed an administrative appeal with the state; when that was turned down, it filed suit against the Department of Natural Resources, arguing that the economic impact on local businesses had not been fully considered. That suit is pending.

The boating speed limits are not the final step. Each county is also required to develop a comprehensive plan for manatee protection. Each plan must address issues such as controls on marina sites and other development.

Despite the increased efforts of recent years, no one is certain that the manatee will thrive in future years. "We'll be able to tell something once the manatee-protection plan starts taking effect," Mr. Turner said. "If we start to see mortality decline, then I have good hope that we can do something. If, after all these efforts, we still see increases in mortality, I really don't know what the next step will be."

Catherine Dold

PEACEFUL UNDERWATER GRAZERS

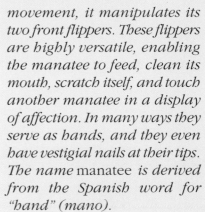

Five hundred years ago Christopher Columbus was sure that he had spotted a group of mermaids in the Caribbean. However, what he actually saw were several manatees coming to the surface for air.

These gentle aquatic mammals live in relatively warm waters, generally over 68° F. The West Indian manatee—the species found in Florida—can survive in both fresh and salt water. It usually swims 3 to 10 feet below the surface, traveling at a leisurely 2 to 5 miles per hour and surfacing to breathe every 4 minutes or so. If necessary, it can speed up to over 15 miles per hour and remain underwater for more than 15 minutes at a time.

To steer and propel itself through the water, the Florida manatee uses its flat tail fin. When it needs to make a precise movement, it manipulates its two front flippers. These flippers are highly versatile, enabling the manatee to feed, clean its mouth, scratch itself, and touch another manatee in a display of affection. In many ways they serve as hands, and they even have vestigial nails at their tips. The name manatee is derived from the Spanish word for "hand" (mano).

Although the Florida manatee is essentially a solitary animal, it may join others when migrating, feeding, or resting. It also likes to play—nibbling, kissing, and embracing other manatees. The only close bond, however, is between a mother and her calf. The calf may continue to nurse for several years, even though it is able to find its own food a month or so after it is born.

Unlike most of the other water mammals, the Florida manatee is a vegetarian. It has a huge appetite and may feed on several hundred pounds of plant matter in just a single day. At one point scientists even tried to put manatees to work, clearing out the water hyacinths that were clogging up Florida's waterways.

On Patrol with an
African Wildlife Warden

Above: *Richard Barnwell has spent much of his working life in Nigeria, where local people hold him in very high esteem.*

Far right: *The leopard is in its element in the Gashaka Gumpti Reserve, where prey animals are abundant.*

F or many, the term *game warden* conjures up an image of a military figure pacing the perimeter of a fenced reserve. The reality is very different. I caught a true glimpse of a warden's life when I talked to Richard Barnwell, who has devoted his career to conserving wildlife. He spent nine years as a game warden in Nigeria and now coordinates the work of conservation projects from the headquarters of the World Wide Fund for Nature (WWF) in England.

Richard's fascination with the outdoors dates back to his childhood in East Africa. One of his earliest memories is of crossing the Serengeti in 1954, when only a single-track road meandered across the vast, empty plains and six lonely huts were the sole sign of human life. It was these haunting images of an Africa teeming with wildlife and relatively undiscovered by today's standards that spurred Richard toward a career in conservation.

Although governments took an increasing interest in "green" issues in the 1970s, ecology was still an unusual career choice at the time. Richard completed one of only two ecological science degrees then available. After he left the university, he began work in Nigeria, starting an association with that country that was to last many years.

Richard's task was to set up the Gashaka Gumpti Reserve, which lies in one of the most remote regions of Nigeria, near the border with Cameroon.

The variety of species it contains makes Gashaka an exciting reserve. Today, troops of up to 50 mona monkeys bound noisily along the branches. At least seven other primate species thrive there, including the Ethiopian colobus monkey, anubis baboon, and white-nosed monkey. The lush forests also conceal some magnificent cats, including the leopard and the golden cat, one of the rarest of the small cats. Grazing herds of antelope, hartebeest, and many gazelle species often stray from the plains into the forests. The more remote uplands of the reserve have not yet been explored, and WWF hopes that it may even find mountain gorillas lurking there.

Before Gashaka Gumpti was established, a series of meetings took place with representatives from the Nigerian government, the local government, and nearby villages. The boundaries of the reserve were first agreed upon on paper, and then local employees marked out the area with piles of stones and steel signs. The game guards also began clearing a 16-foot strip of vegetation to act as a buffer zone around the boundary of the reserve.

Richard learned the language so that he could explain to local people the reasons for conservation work and the benefits of living within a conservation area. One of his first tasks was to employ villagers to build roads across the reserve, with access monitored at a single entry point.

Right: *The Defassa waterbuck has an oily coat, which helps it deal with its wet habitat.*

It was hoped that if poaching could be fully eradicated in Gashaka, animals such as Derby's giant eland (an unusual species of antelope) might be enticed to cross the Cameroon border and return to their old haunts. The new roads also allowed game guards to move swiftly through the reserve in pursuit of poachers and enabled local people to transport produce for the first time to sell in neighboring villages.

Although planning for local people has become commonplace in the 1990s, the establishment of Gashaka represented a new approach. Richard explains the shift in attitude: "In the 1950s game wardens concentrated on policing the reserves, but today a greater emphasis is placed on maintaining a good rapport with local people."

He still has fond memories of the time he spent in Gashaka. "The seven years in Nigeria were the most challenging of my career. It was a real pioneering job going out into an area where very little development had taken place and lifestyles hadn't changed for centuries. Relating to people from a 20th-century vantage point involved crossing an enormous cultural bridge."

For Richard, this meant being accepted by a population whose beliefs were largely animistic. "There is a whole spirit world out there which we have no insight into. For them it's a very real world—even the most mentally well-put-together person will talk to you very seriously about the spirits."

When Richard chose a secluded patch of forest in which to build his home, the local people warned him that a village had once occupied the site. Since the dead were usually buried in back gardens, the site was believed to be full of spirits. Despite the

Below: *Hippopotamuses are widespread in central Africa. They usually spend the day resting in or near a river or pool of water.*

warnings, Richard went ahead and built the house. He discovered that this was interpreted as an extraordinary ease with the spirit world, and stories circulated that he actually talked to the spirits. When several notorious poachers coincidentally died in accidents, Richard assumed supernatural powers in the eyes of the locals, and he became known as the "man with magic."

Although poachers are clearly a menace, there is often a need for wardens to kill animals within the reserve. This may appear to be at odds with the aims of conservation, but reserves are often so successful that animal numbers escalate and must be controlled. "At Gashaka baboons and monkeys were trampling the crops of local farmers. To let the farmers destroy the animals themselves would have been shirking my responsibility," Richard explains.

Today, the wildlife project managers have had their role widened to include research work and the training of local staff. Many game wardens, such as those working in Tanzania, spend much of their time attending government meetings, where they put forward their case for the preservation of national parks.

When he was in Nigeria, Richard devoted much of his time to patrolling with the game guards. "There can be a tendency for the senior officer to stay in the office while the game guards patrol a reserve," he recalls. "This method never works and I feel that you must have people who will go out in the field; it immediately boosts morale." He believes that leadership is the key to success. "A passionate commitment to conservation projects is not enough; you must be adaptable. It's no use having people that are so obsessed with what they do that they fall apart at the first hurdle."

For Richard and other workers at WWF, enduring the political upheavals of countries like Ethiopia has been both frustrating and disappointing. "Until the war in the north of the country stopped it was pointless," he says. "All we were doing was allowing the Ethiopian government to divert more funds into fighting a ridiculous war."

Above: *The secretary bird is a peculiarly long-legged bird of prey that kills and eats snakes.*

*Right: **The needs of migratory animals such as wildebeest present a special challenge to a game park, with its artificial boundaries.***

*Below: **Buffalo do so well in Gashaka that game wardens must often cull a few to control the numbers.***

While working on a farming project with WWF in Somalia, the Barnwell family found themselves living in a police state as the civil war escalated. "Many of the roads were mined and avoiding being blown up became a daily task. Each day you heard of someone falling victim to a road mine." Months of planning and hard work were undone in a bombing raid by the Somali air force. The planes flattened a dam that Richard's conservation project had been building to contain water for irrigation.

Despite these setbacks, Richard has always persevered to ensure that his conservation projects are a success. In Ethiopia he worked on a project funded by the European Community to improve peasant agri-

servation projects and drawing up new plans. These proposals must pass through government committees if they are to receive funds. Although he spends much of his time on paperwork, he also makes essential visits to the field to offer advice.

Richard hopes that Gashaka will become as big an attraction as Cameroon's Korup National Park. One of the few parks to combine forest and savanna, Gashaka offers many options for tourists. They can sample the sights of the rainforest on foot or ride in jeeps through open grasslands. Richard is enthusiastic: "We are rebuilding the infrastructure, retraining the staff, and education and conservation programs are under way for all the villages—education will be the major thrust of the new phase."

In Gashaka, a school is usually little more than a hut, and a blackboard may be the only teaching aid available. WWF aims to improve conditions and to provide educational materials that focus on local conservation projects. It is all a part of the new initiatives that Richard has seen in his time working in the field, helping humans and wildlife to live in harmony with each other.

Suzanne Jones

culture. "We imported over 165,000 tons of fertilizer each year. Farmers knew that using it would improve their yields and were using it almost continuously."

This source of aid actually did more harm than good. "The farmers were becoming trapped in a cycle of fertilizer dependency," Richard explains. "No other work was being done on green manuring or crop rotation, or on teaching them how to use their own resources. All their hopes were pinned on buying fertilizer, and when the money ran out they were going to be left high and dry."

Richard's latest job at WWF headquarters has taken him back to Gashaka. He now coordinates projects in Africa, dividing his time between reporting on existing con-

Left: *Baboons form close-knit communities in the forests. They have a tendency to raid crop fields, however, and game wardens must manage them carefully.*

UPDATE ON '92

NEW LEASE ON LIFE FOR PANDAS

In January 1992, after two years of discussion regarding an ambitious World Wide Fund for Nature (WWF) plan to add 14 more reserves for the giant panda, the Chinese government promised more than $1.5 million to establish the first 4 reserves. This is an important step, since the captive breeding program carried out in the 1980s had lost its momentum. Ironically, however, after producing only one short-lived panda in 10 years, the Wolong Center produced twins in September 1991. The money that has been pledged by the Chinese government will also be used to fund projects to encourage the forestry industry to stop logging in the reserve areas and to encourage local villagers to carry out sustainable agriculture outside the reserves.

WWF is, in the long term, looking for an investment of nearer $75 million to fund the entire project.

CONDORS FLYING FREE

After five years during which no California condors flew over the mountains of Southern California, these magnificent birds of prey may once again be seen in their natural habitat. In 1987 the last of the wild condors was captured in an attempt to save the species from extinction. Scientists had pinned all their hopes on a controversial captive breeding program. Fortunately, by the end of 1991 numbers in the zoos involved had risen from 27 to 51, and a care-ful reintroduction to the wild was possible. Two eight-month-old birds were released in mid-January 1992. Although one was found dead in October, the other is reported to be doing well. It is hoped that captive-bred condors will continue to be released until two separate wild populations exist, each consisting of 100 birds.

KING CHEETAH FOUND

The king cheetah is a handsome and extremely rare variant of the common cheetah, with an impressive black-and-gold leopardlike coat. The only sightings of this big cat had been in southern Africa until recently, when a skin was recovered from a poacher from Burkina-Faso in West Africa.

NEW SPECIES COME TO LIGHT

A number of new animals appear to have been discovered following the exploration of the remote Vu Quang nature reserve in western Vietnam. During a survey organized by the WFF and the Vietnamese Forestry Ministry, a large dagger-horned, goatlike mammal, several fish, a sunbird, and a new race of yellow box tortoise were found. The discovery of the "goat" is particularly exciting, since few large mammals have been discovered this century.

GIANT CLAMS SAVED

Operation Clamsaver, a project based at Orpheus Island in Queensland, Australia, has been a huge success. Eight Pacific nations took part in the project to conserve several species of giant clam. After only seven years, however, the researchers found that they had reared over 90,000 clams and had to ask the navy to help move the huge bivalves to suitable reintroduction sites. The clams were kept in children's wading pools on the decks of ships during the trip to their new homes.

EUROPEAN AGREEMENT ON BATS

On December 4, 1991, an agreement pertaining to the conservation of bats in Europe was signed under the Bonn Convention. This agreement is designed to help conserve a network of safe roosts and feeding sites for all 30 species of European bat, many of which have declined dramatically in recent years. In the fall of 1991 the mouse-eared bat was officially declared extinct in Great Britain. A single male had been in existence at one site in southern Britain, but it failed to make an appearance in 1991.

NORTH SEA DOLPHINS TOO . . .

A new agreement under the Bonn Convention was signed by Britain in May 1992 to help promote the conservation of small cetaceans—dolphins and porpoises—in the North Sea. The main threats to these sea mammals appear to come from pollution, disease, and accidental entrapment in fishing nets. One of the first tasks undertaken as a result of the agreement will be an attempt to collate more comprehensive information about cetacean populations. This data will lead to suggestions about how cetacean conservation can best be approached.

BRITISH BIRDS DECLINE

According to surveys by the British Trust for Ornithology, there was a significant fall in the breeding rate of Great Britain's main bird species during 1991. Breeding numbers of the tawny owl were the lowest since the surveys began in 1963. This drop may be the result of a decline in the populations of the owl's prey species—mice, voles, and other small mammals. Other bird species suffering the decline included the wren, whitethroat, robin, blackcap, blackbird, and song thrush. The chaffinch was the only species for which an increase in the breeding rate was recorded. This increase was probably due to a heavy crop of beech mast, which the chaffinch eats.

NEW ATTEMPTS TO SAVE SIBERIAN CRANE

The Indian wintering population of the Siberian crane continues to balance perilously on the brink of extinction. Large numbers of the rare bird are believed to have been shot as they flew north to their summer breeding grounds, and only four Siberian cranes overwintered in India between 1991 and 1992.

In the early part of 1992 Russian conservationists released 11 captive-bred chicks along the River Ob in the western Siberian plains, part of the crane's migration route. If the Indian population of the Siberian crane becomes extinct in spite of these efforts, attempts will then be made to release a number of captive-bred Siberian cranes into the common crane's breeding grounds. It is then hoped that the birds will be guided back to India when the common cranes migrate.

ENVIRONMENTAL ISSUES

WETLANDS THREAT

The cattle-free status of the great Okavango Delta in Botswana may soon be under threat. Cattle generate both prestige and wealth for local farmers. Already almost half the population is involved in cattle-rearing, and the country has reached its full cattle-carrying capacity. The number of cattle used to be kept in check by disease that was carried by the tsetse fly, which invaded the region in 1925. But modern methods of fly eradication have opened up the possibility of grazing in the Okavango Delta, one of the world's most important wetland sites. However, conservationists have so far been successful in persuading the government to keep the Okavango Delta cattle-free. Fear of foot-and-mouth disease spreading from the wild population to domestic animals has led to the erection of a fence, which now surrounds the delta to the south and will soon extend up the northern banks of the Okavango River, which feeds the delta.

The erection of the fence has led to unexpected conflicts. In addition to its role in controlling disease, the fence serves to keep cattle out of the delta's grazing lands. In spite of the severe drought affecting southern Africa, the water level in the delta is at its highest in 20 years, so cattle farmers are looking with increasing anger at the grazing set aside for wildlife. Local peoples that used to graze cattle in the delta before the advent of the tsetse fly claim that they are being kept out of traditional grazing lands. However, the loss of their cattle has led many people to take up a hunter-gatherer lifestyle. While the vital natural resources on which they depend would be lost if cattle grazing were extended deep into the delta, the fence itself is keeping these people out of many areas on which they depend for food. It is also causing the death of many wild animals by interfering with their traditional migration routes. A government fact-finding team is currently investigating the various arguments. The team's findings will almost certainly influence the government's land use and development plan for the Okavango.

RHINOS STILL THREATENED

Despite hopes in recent years that the trade in rhinoceros horns from Africa had been abating, recent reports indicate that there has in fact been a large increase. There are believed to be fewer than 3,500 black rhinos left in the wild. One major dagger producer in Yemen, where rhino horns are carved to make ornate handles on the weapons, has recently imported over 1,650 pounds of horn believed to have come from at least 260 rhinos. The bulk of the horn appears to come from Zimbabwe, where the government has recently responded with a program to dehorn its remaining black rhinos in an attempt to deter poachers—the major culprits.

CITES MEETING '92

In March 1992, the Convention on International Trade in Endangered Species (CITES) met in Kyoto in Japan. One of the main issues was the global ban on trade in elephant ivory that was imposed by CITES in 1989. Four South African countries —Botswana, Malawi, Zimbabwe, and

Namibia—wanted to allow limited trade of elephant products, including ivory, on the basis that wildlife should pay for its keep. However, at the Convention, overwhelming pressure from other African countries forced these nations to withdraw their proposals. In spite of this, the controversy surrounding the "farming" of wildlife is far from resolved and will remain a major area of disagreement in the future.

Also at the meeting were strong campaigns from organizations like the Royal Society for the Protection of Birds (RSPB) to ban the import of wild-caught bird species for the pet trade and, more specifically, trade in parrots. It was agreed that countries should keep records of bird deaths in transit and suspend trade in species that suffer significant mortality. However, there was some argument over the definition of "significant" in this context, and the United Kingdom proposed far lower levels than those that the Convention finally accepted. There were also no clear moves to curtail the overall trade in wild birds. The RSPB is trying to draw attention to airlines that are still involved in transporting wild-caught birds.

POLLUTION OF WAR–THE GULF

Over a year after the environmental disaster in Kuwait resulting from the Gulf War, all the burning oil wells have been extinguished, but the landscape is still scarred with treacherous oil lakes. Some of these have begun to harden, but the centers are still liquid, luring unsuspecting birds and insects to their death. The Gulf is an important flyway for migrating birds, many of which are fatally attracted to these

"lakes" because they appear to be filled with water. Resident species of desert bird have been heavily sooted by the smoke from burning wells. But colonies of terns and other seabird species nesting farther south in the Gulf may not have been as badly affected as was initially feared.

A longer-term problem is the pollution of the groundwaters in Kuwait. It is estimated that almost two billion gallons of seawater were used to put out the fires, and this depletion could now seriously affect vital freshwater supplies. There are also threats to the sea mammals in the Gulf. Of special concern is the long-term effects of oil slicks on the endangered dugong, which feeds on sea grasses in the shallow waters.

TIGER POACHING CONTINUES

Poachers have sustained their hunting of tigers in the Indian reserve of Ranthambhor, the flagship of the WWF-sponsored recovery operation Project Tiger. Tiger numbers have dropped from 44 to 15 during the last three years, in spite of a CITES ban on trade in tiger products. The increase in poaching is linked to the growing demand for tiger bone as a medical remedy in Japan, South Korea, and Taiwan.

WILDLIFE AND CONSERVATION ORGANIZATIONS

ICELAND LEAVES IWC

In February Iceland gave notice that it would leave the International Whaling Commission (IWC). Iceland announced its withdrawal after a request to take 92 fin and 158 minke whales was turned down. It says that the IWC has changed from being an

organization founded for the conservation and exploitation of whales to becoming purely a conservation organization. There has been an IWC ban on commercial whaling since 1986. Since the ban was upheld by the IWC at its meeting in July, Iceland formally withdrew from the Commission and, along with Norway, announced its intention of resuming commercial whale hunting. Norway also declared its intention to begin a three-year scientific research program in July 1992, which will involve killing nearly 400 minke whales.

Before the meeting, the IWC's scientific committee had said that the population of minke whales had recovered sufficiently to allow the reintroduction of controlled commercial hunting of the species.

The European Community (EC) aims to join the IWC to ensure that IWC rules are enshrined in EC law. If Norway continues whaling, it could be ineligible for EC membership.

RIVER DOLPHIN NUMBERS CONTINUE TO DECLINE

The baiji, or Yangtze River, dolphin in China continues to decline, mainly as a result of entanglement with fishing gear and the destructive results of human disturbance. Its total population has now been estimated at fewer than 300. The Whale and Dolphin Conservation Society (WDCS) is funding research and conservation work to attempt to halt the decline of this endangered mammal and is also introducing educational programs for local people to inform them of the importance of the dolphins. The WDCS is also funding research into the equally threatened river dolphins in the Amazon.

DOLPHIN-DEADLY OR DOLPHIN-FRIENDLY TUNA

Following protests in the United States and the United Kingdom at the revelation that millions of dolphins had been killed in the process of fishing for yellow-fin tuna, the tuna industry announced agreements to move toward using "dolphin-friendly" tuna. In the fall of 1991 over three-quarters of the U.K.'s tuna industry signed an agreement after nearly a year of negotiations with the Whale and Dolphin Conservation Society.

However, the monitoring and implementation of the agreement have been patchy. Some companies have installed cannery inspectors, while others are simply taking their suppliers' word that the tuna are caught using "dolphin-friendly" methods like long-lining or pole and line fishing. Conservation organizations feel that for the agreement to be effective, observers must be placed at locations where it is possible that drift-net-caught "dolphin-deadly" tuna could be disguised as "dolphin-friendly." Until that time, claims made by the various companies cannot be absolutely validated.

ILLEGAL BIRD TRADE KILLS UNKNOWN SPECIES

The Environmental Investigation Agency brought to light the case of four birds of a previously unknown species that were found dead in a bird trader's cage in Tanzania. The captives were to be sold as pets in the European Community (EC). Although it is illegal for wild birds to be sold in the EC as well as in Japan and the United States, no action has been taken in any of these countries to stop the trade, which results in the death of three out of four birds during their transit in what are often cramped and cruel conditions.

TRAFFIC CONDEMNS GREEK WILDLIFE TRADE

TRAFFIC, the wildlife monitoring agency, found hundreds of tourist shops on Greek islands selling wildlife products from endangered species. As a result of TRAFFIC's report, the WWF condemned the Greek government for allowing trade in endangered species to flourish. Greece is not a signatory to CITES, which has banned the trade in objects made of jaguar and cheetah skin, sea turtle shells, ivory trinkets, and stuffed rare birds, all of which TRAFFIC found in the tourist shops. But as a member of the European Community, Greece is obliged to implement any decisions made by CITES and should not allow trade to continue.

THE COMMUNICATORS AND EDUCATORS

ATTENBOROUGH LAUNCHES WATER GROUP

Sir David Attenborough is the head of a new British organization, Water for Wildlife, launched early this year. The group is dedicated to campaigning for increased powers for the National Rivers Authority (NRA) and for awareness of the need for water conservation and recycling, which is especially important as drought conditions hit Great Britain once again. By raising public awareness and by bringing changes to the NRA, Water for Wildlife hopes to benefit the many species that have declined as a result of drought, overextraction, and pollution in Britain's rivers. These include swans, kingfishers, mayflies, and dragonflies.

BELLAMY SIGNS MAGNA CARTA

To commemorate the 777th anniversary in June of the signing of the Magna Carta, the Conservation Foundation, led by David Bellamy, produced a New Magna Carta. This was drawn up to declare a commitment to Britain's living heritage, and the celebrity signatories—Bellamy, Robert Hardy, Sir George Trevelyan, and Allen Meredith—signed the document underneath an ancient yew tree near the historic site at Runnymede, where the original Magna Carta was signed.

The Conservation Foundation encouraged people across the country to organize their own local ceremonies where they could read the New Magna Carta aloud and take an oath to support the environmental pledges that it lists. These pledges include a promise to use 50 percent less energy and never to disturb natural environments or their wildlife. The document, which was written by David Bellamy, also contains a pledge that Britain "will lead, not trail our fellow members of the expanding Europe when it comes to woodlands, forests, and forestry."

Money raised from selling copies of the New Magna Carta—some of which are in Latin—will be channeled into the Yew Tree Campaign for preserving Britain's ancient yew trees. The Conservation Foundation also intends to produce a gazette chronicling the age and location of these ancient trees throughout the United Kingdom, using information gathered from volunteers.

CALENDAR OF EVENTS

Indigenous peoples from Alaska form a coalition with the aim of persuading the scientific establishment to use their traditional methods of observing and understanding the natural world. They are particularly concerned about the decline of species in the Bering Sea.

Hundreds of dead or dying dolphins are washing up on the shores of Turkey and Greece, victims of what may be the latest phase of a viral epidemic that has afflicted marine mammals in the Mediterranean since 1990. The virus destroys the dolphins' immune system, making the animals vulnerable to other diseases. Some scientists believe water pollutants play a role in these epidemics by weakening the dolphins' immune system.

10 The Nature Conservancy and a local conservation organization purchase 143,000 acres of rainforest in eastern Paraguay to create the Mbaracayú Forest Nature Reserve.

16 Corporate leaders from around the world meet in California for Synergy '92, "Building the Sustainable Corporation," a two-day conference convened by the National Wildlife Federation and other organizations to discuss environmentally sustainable economic development.

18 The United Nations Intergovernmental Panel on Climate Change (IPCC) says that pollution seems to be slowing the man-made global warming effect. However, this atmospheric cooling is only likely to delay the warming by a few years.

At a meeting in Penang, Indonesia, representatives of over 50 indigenous peoples from tropical forests worldwide form the International Alliance of the Indigenous Tribal Peoples of the Tropical Forests. The group issues a charter declaring its members' rights to self-determination and control over their lands and resources and condemning destruction of their forests.

Congress passes legislation to create the Salt River Bay National Historic Park and Ecological Preserve in St. Croix in the U.S. Virgin Islands. Although only 912 acres in size, the preserve is a unique geologic and marine area that provides vital habitat for over a hundred bird species, including 24 that are endangered, and 3 endangered sea turtle species. The park is also a warbler and thrush migration stopover.

9 Nearly 2,000 conservationists from around the world meet in Caracas, Venezuela, for the Fourth World Congress on National Parks and Protected Areas. Sponsored once every decade by the World Conservation Union, the congress addresses problems facing parks and develops new conservation strategies.

11 President Bush orders U.S. manufacturers to end virtually all production of chemicals that damage the earth's protective ozone layer by December 31, 1995.

11 The Global Biodiversity Strategy is launched by the World Conservation Union, the United Nations Environment Programme, and the World Resources Institute. It suggests that Third World countries declare ownership of their resources as a way of protecting the earth's diversity of species while allowing those countries to profit from the growing demand for their plants and animals.

20 The World Wide Fund for Nature publishes a study on the effects of global warming on national parks and protected areas around the world. The report states that half of the plant and animal life in these areas is at risk.

A report for the International Council for Bird Preservation details the damages to wildlife arising from the fighting in Croatia. Birds, fish, and mammals are threatened as a result of the conflict.

In the Mediterranean, an alien species of seaweed spreads through the waters of the French and Italian rivieras and threatens to overwhelm native sea grass, which is an important breeding ground for fish.

The World Resources Institute reports that since World War II, eleven percent of the earth's vegetated surface has lost most of its biological productivity. Most of this soil destruction is attributed to overgrazing, poor agricultural practices, and deforestation.

3 The Michigan Scenic Rivers Act is signed into law, designating 14 rivers on U.S. Forest Service land in Michigan for protection. The designation prohibits federal permits for or funding of dams or other development that could harm these rivers.

13 A 12-day conference on the Convention on International Trade in Endangered Species (CITES) concludes, with mixed results. Delegates at the Kyoto, Japan, meeting voted to continue a ban on trade in ivory and other elephant products (see *Update on '92,* page 195), to restrict trade in American black bear parts, and to maintain trade restrictions for the leopard and black rhino. However, no action was taken to curb poaching of rhino species, and several initiatives to restrict trade in endangered species were blocked.

27 New York State Governor Mario Cuomo cancels a $17 billion, 20-year contract to purchase power from Hydro-Quebec, the provincially owned utility of Quebec, Canada. The governor decided that reduced energy demand and energy conservation measures made the contract unnecessary. The planned project would alter the flow of 19 rivers, destroying wilderness and flooding the ancestral homelands of native peoples.

APRIL '92

Norway and Russia raise their seal hunt quota from 51,000 to 60,000. Greenpeace protests that there is no scientific justification for the increase.

The prolonged drought in southern Africa is beginning to kill large numbers of animals in southeastern Zimbabwe. The hippopotamuses of Gonarezhou National Park may become extinct as a result, and elephant, kudu, and eland populations are also at risk.

The Columbia and Snake rivers, whose salmon stocks have been damaged by huge dams and pollution, are declared the most endangered in America by the conservation organization American Rivers.

6 An aye-aye (a rare type of lemur) is born at Duke University Primate Center in North Carolina. It is the first aye-aye born in captivity outside Madagascar, its native home. The aye-aye is considered the most endangered primate in the world.

16 The Exxon Valdez oil spill in March 1989 caused far more damage to animals and resources in Prince William Sound than was previously thought, according to a report released by the Exxon Valdez Oil Spill Trustee Council, a group of federal and state officials overseeing the spill restoration effort. The report describes extensive damage to sea otters, killer whales, harbor seals, seabirds, and fish and concludes that oil remaining in the Sound continues to damage the ecosystem.

20 The U.S. Fish and Wildlife Service issues a permit to the Columbus Zoo in Ohio to import two giant pandas from China for a short-term exhibition, despite objections from the World Wildlife Fund (WWF) and other groups. "Disrupting and dislocating pandas for largely commercial ends will do nothing to enhance the survival of this critically endangered species," said WWF Senior Vice President Jim Leape.

22 Earth Day is observed throughout the United States. Highlighting the events this year were tree-planting projects undertaken by 200 Global Releaf groups nationwide.

29 The world's population is expected to rise from 5.48 billion in mid-1992 to 10 billion in 2050 before leveling off at 11.6 billion after 2150, according to the latest projections of the United Nations Population Fund. The UN agency called for a "sustained and concerted program" to curb the population expansion and avoid increased poverty, hunger, and strain on the earth's natural resources.

MAY '92

The world's space nations agree to a joint program utilizing new satellites and a dozen existing satellites to measure global environmental changes.

Interior Secretary Manuel Lujan convenes a special committee that exempts 13 Bureau of Land Management old-growth timber sale areas in Oregon from the Endangered Species Act, permitting logging even though the forests provide habitat for the threatened northern spotted owl. Environmental groups take the committee to court, arguing that its decision is illegal.

17 President Bush agrees to allow companies to increase emissions of pollutants without notifying the public, despite the opposition of Environmental Protection Agency administrator William K. Reilly.

18 A World Bank report states that educating women is the most productive investment in solving problems of poverty and environmental destruction, as educated women are better able to learn about birth control options and are more likely to have fewer and healthier children.

21 One of Rwanda's endangered mountain gorillas is killed in the Rwandan Volcanoes National Park when caught in a crossfire between Rwandan government troops and the rebel Rwandan Patriotic Front. Only about 600 mountain gorillas remain in the wild.

29 Two leopard-cat kittens are born at New York's Bronx Zoo in the first successful artificial insemination of a wild cat. The event is a breakthrough in efforts to breed captive rare cat species and help prevent their extinction.

JUNE '92

Local authorities in Hargeisa, Somalia's second largest city, appeal for international aid when deadly pesticides leach into their water supplies. These chemicals came from the operations base of East Africa's Desert Locust Control Organization, which was abandoned in 1988 as a result of the country's civil war.

The United Nations Earth Summit takes place in Rio de Janeiro. See the feature on page 74 for details.

10 Satellite photos of the Pacific Northwest that were taken by scientists from the National Aeronautics and Space Administration's Goddard Space Flight Center show severe fragmentation of the region's forests due to clearcutting. The researchers say the region is so fragmented that the overall health of the forest is in jeopardy.

18 After protests from the World Conservation Union and local people, the government of Botswana cancels an intended major dredging program in the Okavango Delta, a site of unique importance to wildlife.

18 Under an accord negotiated by the Inter-American Tropical Tuna Commission, the 10 nations that take 99 percent of the tuna catch in the eastern Pacific agree to reduce the number of dolphins killed in tuna nets by 80 percent by the end of the decade. Signing the agreement were Costa Rica, France, Japan, Nicaragua, Mexico, Panama, Spain, the United States, Venezuela, and Vanuatu.

29 The U.S. Supreme Court issues a ruling in a closely watched land-use case brought by South Carolina developer David Lucas, who was prevented from building on property he owned by a beachfront-protection law and demanded compensation. The court reaffirms states' rights to regulate land use to protect public health and the environment, but holds that if a regulation deprives a landowner of all of the value from a property, the owner deserves compensation. The case is sent back to a South Carolina court to determine if Lucas has lost 100 percent of the value of his property.

JULY '92

Hundreds of dolphins have reportedly drowned in the Mediterranean after being trapped in drift nets used by South Korean fishing vessels to catch tuna and swordfish.

Former Soviet president Mikhail Gorbachev is to head "Green Cross," a new organization that aims to be the environmental equivalent of the Red Cross.

3 The annual International Whaling Commission (IWC) conference, held in Scotland, concludes with a decision to maintain the six-year-old ban on commercial whaling for another year. (See *Update on '92*, page 196, for details.)

6 Scientists declare that only 3 species of fish now inhabit Africa's Lake Victoria, compared with 38 in the 1970s. Researchers blame this development on the introduction in 1960 of the Nile perch, which preys so voraciously on smaller fish that it has disrupted the lake's food chain. Algae normally eaten and kept in check by the smaller fish have multiplied, robbing the water of oxygen and thus making the lake's lower depths uninhabitable.

11 The Canadian government prohibits cod fishing on the Grand Banks off Newfoundland and Labrador, where numbers of spawning cod are among the lowest ever recorded.

AUGUST '92

A major logging, pulp, and paper project planned for the Merauké area of Irian Jaya, Indonesia, may be abandoned following the withdrawal of one of the two companies supporting it. The project would have involved the clearcutting of nearly two million acres of tropical forest and its replacement by eucalyptus plantations. After the project was denounced as disastrous for the environment and the local Auyu forest people, PT Astra, Indonesia's second largest company, pulled out.

A number of California's most renowned bathing beaches are closed due to pollution from coliform bacteria—a result of untreated sewage leaking into offshore waters.

24 Hurricane Andrew—the third worst hurricane to hit the United States this century, slams into the south Florida coast, causing extensive damage to the region, including the 1.4-million-acre Everglades National Park. Early indications are that most endangered animal species in the area survived the storm. But scientists fear that millions of native plants destroyed by the storm may be replaced by quick-growing foreign species.

SEPTEMBER '92

Scientists at the National Oceanic and Atmospheric Administration in Boulder, Colorado, announce that ozone depletion over Antarctica is occurring earlier and faster than in 1991. Readings over the South Pole this month were 15 percent lower than similar readings taken the same week last year. It is unclear whether this accelerated depletion has natural or man-made causes.

18 Scientists at the Univeristy of Basal in Switzerland report that an increase of carbon dioxide in the earth's atmosphere may be more damaging to plants than was previously believed, and current levels may already be harmful. Research suggests that excessive carbon dioxide impairs photosynthesis, the process by which plants create and store fuel. Rising carbon dioxide levels anticipated in the next 100 years could thus not only contribute to warmer global temperatures but also injure plants—not help them grow, as some scientists have argued.

28 The U.S. Fish and Wildlife Service adds the marbled murrelet, a seabird, to the list of threatened species, making it illegal to harm the bird and requiring the federal government to make efforts to protect it, under the Endangered Species Act. The decision may lead to more logging restrictions in the Pacific Northwest, where the bird nests and breeds.

OCTOBER '92

Biologists report a severe decline in the number of monarch butterflies migrating from the eastern United States south to Mexico this fall. While the cause of the decline is uncertain, it may stem from the severe 1991 winter at the monarch's roosting sites in Mexico. Conservationists fear that this year's scarcity of butterflies may signal trouble for the species, whose habitat is shrinking in the United States and Mexico.

Congress authorizes almost two million dollars for the continued restoration of Florida's Kissimmee River. In a project sponsored by the state of Florida, the U.S. Army Corps of Engineers will refill a canal it constructed and allow the river to reform its original curves, restoring thousands of acres of the ecosystem. It is hoped that hundreds of animal species will reinhabit the region, including endangered species such as bald eagles and Florida panthers.

5 Start of International Elephant Week, which celebrates the 1989 ban on trade in elephant ivory.

17 The sixth annual World Rainforest Week begins, sponsored by the Rainforest Action Network in coordination with other environmental groups. The theme for the week is the General Agreement on Tariffs and Trade (GATT) and the potential of liberalized trade rules to adversely affect rainforests by undermining environmental laws of the United States and other nations.

23 Legislation to greatly reduce the importation of rare exotic birds to the United States is signed into law by President Bush. The U.S. Fish and Wildlife Service will prohibit imports of the birds regardless of documentation issued by an exporting nation.

26 The Environmental Protection Agency issues the first of several new clean-air rules, establishing regulations that will cut in half the permissible emissions of acid rain-causing sulfur dioxide by the year 2010. The rule also permits utilities to buy and sell pollution allowances.

30 Scientists report the discovery of the first known poisonous bird—the hooded pitohui, which is native to New Guinea. Although the bird's existence was already known, biologists have just learned that its feathers and skin harbor a potent toxin that appears to repel predators.

NOVEMBER '92

A Montreal Protocol meeting on protecting the ozone layer is held in Copenhagen, Denmark, and attended by representatives from the world's industrialized and developing nations. Major topics of debate include chlorofluorocarbons, halons, and other ozone-depleting chemicals.

2 President Bush signs drift-net legislation that imposes trade penalties on nations that fish with drift nets in the North Pacific in 1993.

DECEMBER '92

Wildlife experts release captive-bred whooping cranes in Florida's Three Lakes Wildlife Management Area. This is the first phase of a 10-year program to reintroduce this endangered species to the wild in Florida, where whooping cranes disappeared more than 60 years ago.

17 The National Audubon Society holds its 93rd Christmas Bird Count, an annual census in which over 40,000 people throughout the Americas count and record all the birds they see. Their data is then analyzed for insights into the health of bird populations.

A GUIDE TO PROTECTED SPECIES

Protection is given to animal species nationally and internationally through laws and treaties. The classification of an animal, as rare or endangered, for example, is important in any attempt to protect it.

IUCN CATEGORIZATION

The World Conservation Union (IUCN) categorizes animals according to the degree to which they are threatened. The IUCN categories are reproduced below.

EXTINCT

Taxa (groups of animals) not definitely located in the wild during the past 50 years (the criterion as used by CITES).

ENDANGERED

Taxa in danger of extinction and whose survival is unlikely if the causal factors continue operating.

Included are taxa whose numbers have been so drastically reduced that they are deemed to be in immediate danger of extinction. Also included are taxa that may be extinct but have definitely been seen in the wild in the past 50 years.

VULNERABLE

Taxa believed likely to move into the "Endangered" category if the causal factors continue operating.

Included are taxa of which most or all the populations are decreasing because of overexploitation, extensive destruction of habitat, or other environmental disturbance; taxa with populations that have been seriously depleted and whose ultimate security has not yet been assured; and taxa with populations that are still abundant but are under threat from severe adverse factors throughout their range.

NOTE: In practice, "Endangered" and "Vulnerable" categories may temporarily include taxa whose populations are beginning to recover as a result of remedial action, but whose recovery is insufficient to justify their transfer to another category.

RARE

Taxa with small world populations that are not presently "Endangered" or "Vulnerable" but that are at risk.

These taxa are usually localized within restricted geographical areas or habitats or are thinly scattered over a more extensive range.

INDETERMINATE

Taxa known to be "Endangered," "Vulnerable," or "Rare" but where there is not enough information to say which of the three categories is appropriate.

INSUFFICIENTLY KNOWN

Taxa that are suspected but not definitely known to belong to any of the above categories, because of lack of information.

COMMERCIALLY THREATENED

Taxa not currently threatened with extinction but most or all of whose populations are threatened as a sustainable commercial resource, or will become so, unless their exploitation is regulated. This category applies only to taxa whose populations are assumed to be relatively large.

CITES

Since 1975, international trade in threatened wildlife and wildlife products has been regulated by the Convention on International Trade in Endangered Species of Wild Fauna and Flora (CITES). The 90 member nations of CITES prohibit or strictly control trade in hundreds of endangered species—both plant and animal. CITES has two main categories of protection: species listed in its Appendix I are threatened with extinction, and trade in them is permitted only in exceptional circumstances. Species in Appendix II are considered potentially endangered by trade—their trade is permitted but is carefully controlled. CITES member nations meet every two years to review the convention and update the lists.

Mammals with Appendix I status are listed on page 203 under their common names. Note that some species or subspecies may not have Appendix I status. In addition, some animals have this status only in certain areas, not their entire range.

CITES APPENDIX I—MAMMALS

Addax
Anoa, lowland
Anoa, mountain
Antelope, giant sable
Antelope, Tibetan
Argali, Tibetan
Armadillo, giant
Ass, African wild
Ass, Asian wild
Avahi (woolly lemurs)
 (all species)
Aye-aye
Babirusa
Bandicoot, barred (long-nosed
 bandicoot)
Bandicoot, bridled nail-tailed
Bandicoot, crescent nail-tailed
Bandicoot, lesser rabbit (Yallara)
Bandicoot, pig-footed
Bandicoot, rabbit (Bilby)
Bear, Asiatic black
Bear, Baluchistan black
Bear, brown
Bear, Mexican grizzly
Bear, red
Bear, spectacled
Bear, sloth
Bear, sun
Bear, Tibetan blue
Bison, woods
Caracal
Cat, Andean
Cat, Asian golden
Cat, black-footed
Cat, flat-headed
Cat, Geoffroy's
Cat, leopard
Cat, marbled
Cat, rusty-spotted
Cat, tiger (little spotted cat)
Chamois, Apennin
Cheetah
Chimpanzee
Chimpanzee, pygmy (bonobo)
Chinchilla (wild)
Colobus, Tana River red
Colobus, Zanzibar red
Deer, Calamianes
Deer, Eld's brow-antlered
Deer, Indochina hog
Deer, Kuhl's (Bawean hog deer)
Deer, marsh
Deer, musk
Deer, pampas
Deer, Persian fallow
Deer, swamp

Dog, bush
Dolphin, Ganges and Indus River
 (all species)
Dolphin, humpback (all species)
Dolphin, white flag (Chinese
 river dolphin)
Drill
Dugong
Duiker, Jentink's
Elephant, African
Elephant, Asiatic
Ferret, black-footed
Flying fox, insular (Tonga
 fruit bat)
Flying fox, Mariana (Mariana
 fruit bat)
Flying fox, Mortlock
Flying fox, Palau
Flying fox, ponape
Flying fox, Samoa
Flying fox, Truk
Gazelle, Dama
Gibbon (all species)
Goral
Gorilla
Hare, hispid (Assam rabbit)
Hog, pygmy
Huemal, North Andean
Huemal, South Andean
Hyena, brown
Indri (all species)
Jaguar
Jaguarundi
Kouprey
Langur, capped
Langur, douc
Langur, golden
Langur, gray (common Indian
 langur)
Langur, long-tailed (Mentawai
 leaf monkey)
Langur, Pagai Island
Langur, snub-nosed (all species)
Lemur (all species)
Lemur, dwarf (all species)
Lemur, fork mouse (fork-marked
 mouse lemur)
Lemur, gentle (all species)
Lemur, hairy-eared dwarf
Lemur, mouse (all species)
Lemur, sportive (weasel lemur)
 (all species)
Leopard
Leopard, clouded
Leopard, snow
Linsang, spotted

Lion, Asiatic (Indian lion)
Lynx, Spanish (Iberian lynx)
Macaque, lion-tailed
Manatee, South American
 (Amazonian manatee)
Manatee, West Indian
Mandrill
Mangabey, Tana River (agile
 mangabey)
Margay
Markhor, Astor
Markhor, Bukhara
Markhor, Chialtan
Markhor, Kabul
Markhor, straight-horned
Marmoset, buff-headed
Marmoset, white-eared
Marsupial mouse, large desert
 (sandhill dunnart)
Marsupial mouse, long-tailed
 (long-tailed dunnart)
Monkey, black-handed spider
Monkey, Diana
Monkey, Goeldi's (callimico)
Monkey, mantled howler
Monkey, proboscis
Monkey, woolly spider
Monkey, yellow-tailed woolly
Mouse, Australian native
 (McDonnell Range rock rat)
Mouse, Shark Bay
Muntjac, black
Ocelet
Ocelet, Brazilian
Orangutan
Oryx, Arabian
Oryx, scimitar-horned
Otter, European
Otter, giant
Otter, long-tailed (neotropical
 otter)
Otter, marine
Otter, southern river (South
 American river otter)
Otter, southern sea
Otter, West African "clawless"
Panda, giant
Pangolin, common African ground
Panther, Florida (Florida puma)
Peccary, Chacoan (giant peccary)
Porpoise, finless
Porpoise, Gulf of California
 harbor (Cochita)
Prairie dog, Mexican
Pronghorn, Baja
Pronghorn, Mexican

Pronghorn, Sonoran
Pudu
Puma, Costa Rican
Puma, Eastern (Adirondack
 cougar)
Rabbit, Mexican volcano
Rat, Australian stick-nest
Rat, false water
Rat-kangaroo (all species in
 genus *Bettongia*)
Rat-kangaroo, desert
Rhinoceros (all species)
Saki, white-nosed
Seal, Guadalupe fur
Seal, monk (all species)
Seladang (gaur)
Serow
Shapo
Siamang
Sifaka (all species)
Squirrel monkey, red-backed
Stag, Kashmir
Tamaraw
Tamarin, cotton-top
Tamarin, golden lion (all species)
Tamarin, pied
Tamarin, white-footed
Tapir, Asian
Tapir, Central American
Tapir, mountain
Tasmanian wolf (Thylacine)
Tiger
Uakari (all species)
Urial
Vicuña
Wallaby, banded hare (Munning)
Wallaby, western hare (Wurrup)
Whale, beaked (all species in
 genus *Berardius*)
Whale, blue
Whale, bottle-nosed (all species)
Whale, bowhead
Whale, Bryde's
Whale, fin
Whale, gray
Whale, humpback
Whale, minke
Whale, pygmy right
Whale, right
Whale, sei
Whale, sperm
Wolf, gray
Wombat, Queensland hairy-nosed
Yak, wild
Zebra, Cape mountain
Zebra, Grevy's

RELATED RESOURCES

BOOKS

Adams, Jonathan, & Thomas McShane. *The Myth of Wild Africa: Conservation Without Illusion.* Norton, 1992.

Allen, Thomas B. *Guardian of the Wild: The Story of the National Wildlife Federation.* Indianapolis University Press, 1987.

Bass, Rick. *The Ninemile Wolves.* Clark City Press, 1992.

Berger, John. *Restoring the Earth: How Americans Are Working to Renew Our Damaged Environment.* Anchor Press, 1987.

Bergman, Charles. *Wild Echoes: Encounters with the Most Endangered Animals in North America.* McGraw-Hill, 1990.

Boyle, Robert H., & R. Alexander Boyle. *Acid Rain.* Schocken Books, 1983.

Brandenburg, Jim. *White Wolf: Living with an Arctic Legend.* Northwood Press, Inc., 1988.

Brown, Lester R., et al. *The World Watch Reader on Global Environmental Issues.* Norton, 1991.

Caufield, Catherine. *In the Rainforest.* University of Chicago Press, 1984.

Dennis, John V. *The Wildlife Gardener.* Knopf, 1985.

DiSilvestro, Roger L. *The Endangered Kingdom.* John Wiley and Sons, 1991.

Domico, Terry, & Mark Newman. *Bears of the World.* Facts on File, 1988.

Durrell, Gerald, with Lee Durrell. *The Amateur Naturalist.* Knopf, 1988.

Durrell, Lee. *State of the Ark: An Atlas of Conservation in Action.* Doubleday, 1986.

Earth Works Group. *50 Simple Things You Can Do to Save the Earth.* Earth Works Press, 1989.

Ehrlich, Paul R., & Anne H. Ehrlich. *Healing the Planet: Strategies for Resolving the Environmental Crisis.* Addison-Wesley, 1991.

Eldredge, Niles. *The Miner's Canary: Unravelling the Mysteries of Extinction.* Simon and Schuster, 1992.

Ellis, Richard. *The Book of Whales.* Knopf, 1985.

Gore, Al. *Earth in the Balance: Ecology and the Human Spirit.* Houghton Mifflin, 1992.

Gould, Stephen Jay. *Ever Since Darwin.* Norton, 1977.

Hall, Bob, & Mary Lee Kerr. *1991-1992 Green Index: A State-by-State Guide to the Nation's Environmental Health.* Island Press, 1991.

Hecht, Suzanne, & Robert Heinzman, eds. *The Fate of the Forest: Developers, Destroyers, and Defenders of the Amazon.* Verso, 1989.

Heintzelman, Donald S. *The Migration of Hawks.* Indiana University Press, 1986.

Lanier-Graham, Susan D. *The Nature Directory: A Guide to Environmental Organizations.* Walker and Company, 1991.

Leatherwood, Stephen, & Randall R. Reeves. *The Sierra Club Handbook of Whales and Dolphins of the World.* Sierra Club Books, 1983.

Lembke, Janet. *Dangerous Birds: A Naturalist's Aviary.* Lyons & Burford, 1992.

Maclean, Norman. *Young Men and Fire.* University of Chicago Press, 1992.

Makower, Joel, ed. *The Nature Catalog.* Vintage Books, 1991.

Marx, Wesley. *The Frail Ocean.* The Globe Pequot Press, 1991.

Matthiessen, Peter. *African Silences.* Random House, 1991.

McKibben, Bill. *The End of Nature.* Anchor Books, 1989.

Mead, Chris. *Bird Migration.* Facts on File, 1992.

Mech, David. *The Wolf.* University of Minnesota Press, 1981.

Miller, Kenton, & Laura Tangley. *Trees of Life: Saving Tropical Forests and Their Biological Wealth.* Beacon, 1991.

Mitchell, Andrew. *The Enchanted Canopy: A Journey of Discovery to the Last Unexplored Frontier, the Roof of the World's Rainforests.* Macmillan, 1983.

Mohlenbrock, Robert H. *Where Have All the Wildflowers Gone? A Region-by-Region Guide to Threatened or Endangered U.S. Wildflowers.* Macmillan, 1983.

Moody, Robert, ed. *The Indigenous Voice: Visions and Realities.* 2 vol. Cultural Survival, 1988.

Naar, John. *Design for a Livable Planet: How You Can Help Clean Up the Environment.* Harper & Row, 1990.

National Geographic Society. *The Emerald Realm: Earth's Precious Rain Forests.* National Geographic Society, 1990.

Newkirk, Ingrid. *Save the Animals! 101 Easy Things You Can Do.* Warner, 1990.

Newman, Arnold. *Tropical Rainforest.* Facts on File, 1990.

Nowak, Ronald M. *Walker's Mammals of the World.* 5th ed. 2 vol. Johns Hopkins University Press, 1991.

Ocko, Stephanie. *Environmental Vacations: Volunteer Projects to Save the Planet.* John Muir Publications, 1992.

Oppenheimer, Michael, & Robert H. Boyle. *Death Heat: The Race Against the Greenhouse Effect.* Basic Books, 1990.

Peck, Robert McCracken. *Land of the Eagle: A Natural History of North America.* Summit Books, 1990.

Piasecki, Bruce, & Peter Asmus. *In Search of Environmental Excellence.* Simon and Schuster, 1990.

Porritt, Jonathan, ed. *Save the Earth.* Turner Publishing, 1991.

Reisner, Mark. *Game Wars: The Undercover Pursuit of Wildlife Poachers.* Viking, 1991.

Revkin, Andrew. *Burning Season: The Murder of Chico Mendes and the Fight for the Amazon Rain Forest.* Houghton Mifflin, 1990.

Rifkin, Jeremy. *Biosphere Politics.* Crown, 1991.

Salathé, Tobias, ed. *Conserving Migratory Birds.* International Council for Bird Preservation, 1991.

Savage, Candace. *Peregrine Falcons.* Sierra Club Books, 1992.

Scarce, Rik. *Eco-Warriors: Understanding the Radical Environmental Movement*. Noble Press, 1990.

Schneider, Stephen H. *Global Warming: Are We Entering the Greenhouse Century?* Sierra Club Books, 1989.

Terborgh, John. *Where Have All the Birds Gone?* Princeton University Press, 1989.

Wilson, Edward O. *The Diversity of Life*. Harvard University Press, 1992.

World Resources Institute. *1992 Information Please Environmental Almanac*. Houghton Mifflin, 1992.

Zuckerman, Seth, with The Wilderness Society. *Saving Our Ancient Forests*. Living Planet Press, 1991.

MAGAZINES & NEWSLETTERS

American Birds. Published by the National Audubon Society.

American Forests. Published by American Forests.

The Amicus Journal. Published by the Natural Resources Defense Council.

Audubon. Published by the National Audubon Society.

Birding. Published by the American Birding Association.

Buzzworm, The Environmental Journal. Published by Buzzworm, Inc.

Cultural Survival Quarterly. Published by Cultural Survival, Inc.

Discover: The World of Science. Published by The Walt Disney Company.

E: The Environmental Magazine. Published by Earth Action Network.

Environmental Action Magazine. Published by Environmental Action, Inc.

Focus. Published by the World Wildlife Fund.

Garbage: The Practical Journal for the Environment. Published by Old House Journal Corp.

Greenpeace. Published by Greenpeace USA.

International Wildlife. Published by the National Wildlife Federation.

Mother Earth News. Published by The Mother Earth News.

National Geographic. Published by National Geographic Society.

National Wildlife. Published by the National Wildlife Federation.

Native Peoples. Published by Media Concepts Group, Inc.

Natural History. Published by the American Museum of Natural History.

Orion Nature Quarterly. Published by Conservation International.

Sierra. Published by the Sierra Club.

Whalewatcher. Published by the American Cetacean Society.

Wildlife Conservation. Published by Wildlife Conservation International.

World Watch. Published by Worldwatch Institute.

CHILDREN'S BOOKS

Earth Works Group. *50 Simple Things Kids Can Do to Save the Earth*. Earth Works Press, 1990.

Earth Works Group. *Kid Heroes of the Environment: Simple Things Real Kids Are Doing to Save the Earth*. Ed. by Catherine Dee. Earth Works Press, 1991.

Fagan, Elizabeth, ed. *Children's Atlas of Wildlife*. Rand McNally, 1990.

Miles, Beverly. *Save the Earth: An Action Handbook for Kids*. Knopf, 1991.

Newkirk, Ingrid. *Kids Can Save the Animals! 101 Easy Things to Do*. Warner, 1991.

Schwartz, Linda. *Earth Book for Kids: Activities to Help Heal the Environment*. Learning Works, 1990.

Stidworthy, John. *Animal Behavior*. The Prentice Hall World of Nature/An Andromeda Book, 1992.

CHILDREN'S MAGAZINES

Dolphin Log. Published by the Cousteau Society.

KIND News (Kids in Nature's Defense Club). Published by the National Association for Humane and Environmental Education.

Planet Three—The Earth-Based Magazine for Kids. Published by P3 Foundation.

Ranger Rick. Published by the National Wildlife Federation.

VIDEOS

The Amazon: A Vanishing Rainforest (1988)

Biodiversity (1988)

Creatures of the Mangrove (1987)

Creatures of the Namib Desert (1986)

The Cry of the Beluga (1989)

For Earth's Sake: The Life and Times of David Brower (1990)

The Great Dinosaur Hunt (1989)

In These Ancient Trees: Effects of Over-logging in the Pacific Northwest (1992)

Ivory Hunters (1990)

The Living Planet (1984; 12-part series)

National Audubon Videos

  Ancient Forests: Rage Over Trees (1989)

  Arctic Refuge: A Vanishing Wilderness (1990)

  California Condor (1986)

  Danger at the Beach (1990)

  Ducks Under Siege (1987)

  Galápagos: My Fragile World (1986)

  Greed & Wildlife: Poaching in America (1989)

  Grizzly & Man: Uneasy Truce (1988)

  If Dolphins Could Talk (1990)

  On the Edge of Extinction: Panthers & Cheetahs (1987)

  Sea Turtles: Ancient Nomads (1988)

  Whales! (1987)

  Wildfire (1990)

  Wolves (1989)

  Wood Stork: Barometer of the Everglades (1987)

National Geographic Videos

  Among the Wild Chimpanzees (1989)

  Elephant (1989)

  Rain Forest (1983)

  Tropical Kingdom of Belize (1985)

  White Wolf (1986)

Nature: Land of the Kiwi (1991)

Nature: Rain Forest (Selva Verde: The Green Jungle) (1990)

NOVA: The Big Spill (1990)

NOVA: In the Land of the Polar Bear (1985)

NOVA: Whale Watch (1987)

Our Threatened Heritage (1988)

The Rainbow Warrior Affair (1989)

Return of the Great Whale (1985)

Save the Earth—A How-To Video (1990)

DIRECTORY OF ORGANIZATIONS

The Acid Rain Foundation, Inc.
1410 Varsity Drive
Raleigh, NC 27606
©(919) 828-9443
Supports research and promotes awareness of acid rain and other atmospheric problems.

The Adirondack Council
P.O. Box D-2
Church St.
Elizabethtown, NY 12932-0640
©(518) 873-2240
Coalition of organizations and individuals that works for the protection of New York State's Adirondack Park through public education, lobbying, and legal action.

Adopt-A-Stream Foundation
P.O. Box 5558
Everett, WA 98201
©(206) 388-3313
Works to protect streams in the U.S. Northwest both for fish habitat and recreational purposes.

African Wildlife Foundation
1717 Massachusetts Ave., NW
Washington, DC 20036
©(202) 265-8393
Works with African nations to protect wildlife through education, wildlife management training, and conservation area management.

Alaska Coalition
408 C St., NE
Washington, DC 20002
©(202) 547-6009
Seeks to preserve Alaska's wild lands through education, research, and lobbying.

American Birding Association
P.O. Box 6599
Colorado Springs, CO 80934
©(800) 634-7736
International organization of birders that promotes recreational birding.

American Cave Conservation Association
Main and Cave St.
P.O. Box 409
Horse Cave, KY 42749
©(502) 786-1466
Protects caves and karstland, along with associated natural resources.

American Cetacean Society
P.O. Box 2639
San Pedro, CA 90731-0943
©(213) 548-6279
Seeks to protect whales and dolphins through research, conservation, and education.

American Forests
1516 P St., NW
Washington, DC 20005
©(202) 667-3300
Works for proper management and use of forests and other natural resources. Sponsors programs such as Global Releaf, an international tree-planting campaign.

American Hiking Society
P.O. Box 20160
Washington, DC 20041-2160
©(703) 385-3252
Protects hiking trails through lobbying, education, and volunteer trail maintenance. Provides an information service for trail users.

American Horse Protection Association
1000 29th St., NW, Ste. T-100
Washington, DC 20007
©(202) 965-0500
Promotes humane treatment of horses and other equines, both wild and domestic.

American Littoral Society
Sandy Hook
Highlands, NJ 07732
©(201) 291-0055
Organization of naturalists seeking to conserve the land and wildlife of shores and adjacent wetlands, bays, and rivers.

American Rivers
801 Pennsylvania Ave., SE, Ste. 303
Washington, DC 20003
©(202) 547-6900
Works to protect rivers and surrounding landscapes through National Wild and Scenic River Act and other laws.

American Society for the Prevention of Cruelty to Animals
441 East 92nd St.
New York, NY 10128
©(212) 876-7700
Seeks to prevent abuse of pets, wild animals, and animals raised for food or used in research and other work.

American Wildlands Alliance
7500 E. Arapahoe Road, Ste. 355
Englewood, CO 80112
©(303) 771-0380
Promotes protection and wise use of wildlands and their resources.

Animal Legal Defense Fund
1363 Lincoln Ave.
San Rafael, CA 94901
©(415) 459-0885
Provides legal services for the protection of animals.

Animal Protection Institute of America
2831 Fruitridge Road
Sacramento, CA 95822
©(916) 422-1921
Works to prevent cruelty to animals and preserve their natural habitats.

Antarctica Project
218 D St., SE
Washington, DC 20003
©(202) 544-2600
Monitors the Antarctic region and lobbies to protect it. Also conducts policy research and provides information to the public.

Appalachian Mountain Club
5 Joy St.
Boston, MA 02108
©(617) 523-0636
Sponsors recreational and conservation programs, such as trail maintenance, in the northeastern U.S.

Audubon Naturalist Society of the Central Atlantic States
8940 Jones Mill Road
Chevy Chase, MD 20815
©(301) 652-9188
Works for the protection of birds, other wildlife, and their habitat. Also sponsors educational and conservation programs.

Bat Conservation International
P.O. Box 162603
Austin, TX 78716
©(512) 327-9721
Works for the protection of bats and their habitats.

California Marine Mammal Center
Marin Headlands
Golden Gate National Recreation Area
Sausalito, CA 94965
©(415) 331-SEAL
Rescues and rehabilitates marine mammals along the Pacific coast.

Canadian Wildlife Federation
1673 Carling Ave.
Ottawa, Ontario
Canada K2A 3Z1
©(613) 725-2191
Works to increase understanding of natural processes. Maintains information and educational programs and conducts and sponsors research.

Caribbean Conservation Corporation
P.O. Box 2866
Gainesville, FL 32602
©(904) 373-6441
Preserves marine turtles in the Caribbean and Atlantic. Conducts sea turtle-tagging program in Costa Rica..

Center for Environmental Information, Inc.
46 Prince St.
Rochester, NY 14607
©(716) 271-3550
Provides information on environmental issues through publications, educational programs, and other types of services.

Center for Marine Conservation
1725 DeSales St., NW, Ste. 500
Washington, DC 20036
©(202) 429-5609
Works for the protection of marine wildlife and habitats. Also works to prevent marine pollution and promote fisheries conservation.

Center for Plant Conservation
P.O. Box 299
St. Louis, MO 63166
©(314) 577-9450
Established to conserve and study rare and endangered plants at U.S. botanical gardens and arboreta.

Charles Darwin Foundation for the Galápagos Isles
National Zoological Park
Washington, DC 20008
©(202) 673-4705
U.S. office of organization that supports protection of the Galápagos Islands through research and scientific education programs.

Citizen's Clearinghouse for Hazardous Wastes
P.O. Box 926
Arlington, VA 22216
©(703) 276-7070
Aids individuals and grass-roots organizations in taking legal action to oppose the unsafe disposal of hazardous wastes.

Clean Ocean Action
P.O. Box 505
Sandy Hook, NJ 07732
©(201) 872-0111
Dedicated to improving the degraded waters off the coasts of New York and New Jersey.

Clean Water Fund
1320 18th St., NW
Washington, DC 20003
©(202) 457-1286
A citizen's group that works for clean, safe water and the protection of wetlands, groundwater, and coastal waters.

Coastal Conservation Association
4801 Woodway, Ste. 220 W.
Houston, TX 77056
©(713) 626-4222
Group of organizations, corporations, and individuals seeking to conserve natural resources of U.S. saltwater coastal areas.

Conservation International
1015 18th St., NW, Ste. 1000
Washington, DC 20036
©(202) 429-5660
Seeks to conserve ecosystems and biological diversity by helping countries implement conservation projects at local levels.

The Cousteau Society
930 W. 21st St.
Norfolk, VA 23517
©(804) 627-1144
An environmental education organization that attempts to improve the quality of life for present and future generations.

Cultural Survival, Inc.
215 First St.
Cambridge, MA 02142
©(617) 621-3818
Supports projects worldwide to help indigenous peoples retain their rights and cultures.

Defenders of Wildlife
1244 19th St., NW
Washington, DC 20036
©(202) 659-9510
Seeks to preserve and protect wildlife and wildlife habitats through education, research, and litigation.

Ducks Unlimited, Inc.
One Waterfowl Way
Long Grove, IL 60047
©(708) 438-4300
Dedicated to conserving North American wetland ecosystems for migratory waterfowl.

Earth Island Institute
300 Broadway, Ste. 28
San Francisco, CA 94133
©(415) 788-3666
Develops a variety of environmental and wildlife protection projects, including the International Marine Mammal Project and the Urban Habitat Program.

Earthwatch
680 Mt. Auburn St.
P.O. Box 403
Watertown, MA 02272
©(617) 926-8200
Arranges for volunteers to work on scientific projects around the world. Projects range from rainforest and endangered species studies to the preservation of archaeological finds.

Elsa Wild Animal Appeal—U.S.A.
P.O. Box 4572
North Hollywood, CA 91617-0572
©(818) 761-8387
Works for the conservation of wildlife and wild places and the establishment of wildlife reserves.

Environmental Action, Inc.
1525 New Hampshire Ave., NW
Washington, DC 20036
©(202) 745-4870
Political action organization that lobbies for strong environmental laws in areas such as pollution prevention. The Environmental Action Foundation is the group's research and education affiliate.

Environmental Defense Fund
257 Park Ave. South
New York, NY 10010
©(212) 505-2100
EDF Hotline: 1-800-CALL-EDF
Organization of lawyers, scientists, and economists working to protect and improve the environment and public health.

Environmental Law Institute
1616 P St., NW, Ste. 200
Washington, DC 20036
©(202) 328-5150
Sponsors research and conferences on environmental law and policy and maintains a clearinghouse for environmental law information.

Environmental Support Center, Inc.
1731 Connecticut Ave., NW,
Ste. 200
Washington, DC 20009
©(202) 328-7813
Assists environmental grass-roots groups with funding for training, equipment, and other needs.

Fauna and Flora Preservation Society
1 Kensington Gore
London SW7 2AR
England, U.K.
071 8238899
Promotes the conservation of wild animals and plants worldwide.

Friends of Animals
11 W. 60th St.
New York, NY 10023
©(212) 247-8120
Works to protect wild, laboratory, and farm animals through breeding control services and other programs.

Friends of the Earth, Environmental Policy Institute, Oceanic Society
218 D St., SE
Washington, DC 20003
©(202) 544-2600
Global advocacy organization that lobbies for responsible use of the earth's resources and publishes information on environmental issues. (The groups merged in 1990.)

The Fund for Animals
200 West 57th St.
New York, NY 10019
©(212) 246-2096
Opposes cruelty to both wild and domestic animals and works to preserve rare species.

Global Tomorrow Coalition
1325 G St., NW, Ste. 915
Washington, DC 20005
©(202) 628-4016
Studies and disseminates information on global problems such as population growth, resource depletion, and unsustainable development.

Great Bear Foundation
P.O. Box 2699
Missoula, MT 59806
©(406) 721-3009
Group of ranchers, loggers, environmentalists, and others working to protect bears of the world.

Greater Yellowstone Coalition
P.O. Box 1874
Bozeman, MT 59771
©(406) 586-1593
Group of organizations formed to preserve the Greater Yellowstone Ecosystem through activism, research, and education.

Greenpeace USA
1436 U St., NW
Washington, DC 20009
©(202) 462-1177
U.S. branch of international organization dedicated to protecting the environment through direct, nonviolent action.

Hawkwatch International
P.O. Box 35706
1420 Carlisle NE, Ste. 100
Albuquerque, NM 87176-5706
©(505) 255-7622
Works to conserve birds of prey in the western U.S. through research and educational programs.

Hawk Mountain Sanctuary Association
Route 2
Kempton, PA 19529
©(215) 756-6961
Maintains refuge for birds of prey and other wildlife and sponsors research to monitor and conserve raptor populations.

The Humane Society of the United States
2100 L St., NW
Washington, DC 20037
©(202) 452-1100
Works to prevent cruelty to wild and domestic animals through investigative work, litigation, public education, and shelter programs.

INFORM
381 Park Ave. South
New York, NY 10016
©(212) 689-4040
Conducts research on hazardous waste, air pollution, and other environmental problems and promotes practical actions to address these issues.

Institute for Conservation Leadership
2000 P St., NW, Ste. 413
Washington, DC 20036
©(202) 466-3330
Provides leadership training and organizational development programs for the environmental community.

Institute for Earth Education
P.O. Box 288
Warrenville, IL 60555
©(509) 395-2299
Works with educators around the world to develop environmental education programs.

International Council for Bird Preservation
32 Cambridge Road
Girton, Cambridge CB3 OPJ
England, U.K.
0223 277318
Campaigns for the protection of birds and their habitats worldwide.

International Fund for Animal Welfare
411 Main St.
P.O. Box 193
Yarmouth Port, MA 02675
©(508) 362-4944
Works for humane treatment of wild and domestic animals.

International Oceanographic Foundation
3979 Rickenbacker Causeway,
Virginia Key
Miami, FL 33149-9900
©(305) 361-4888
Provides information on and encourages scientific study of oceans.

International Primate Protection League
P.O. Box 766
Summerville, SC 29484
©(803) 871-7988
Works to protect primates worldwide. Investigates illegal trafficking and supports sanctuaries and rehabilitation projects.

International Rivers Network
301 Broadway, Ste. B
San Francisco, CA 94133
©(415) 986-4694
Group of organizations, activists, and professionals that promotes responsible water policies and projects worldwide.

International Wildlife Coalition
634 N. Falmouth Hwy.
P.O. Box 388
N. Falmouth, MA 02556
©(508) 564-9980
Works for the preservation of wildlife and wildlife habitats.

Izaak Walton League of America
1401 Wilson Blvd. Level B
Arlington, VA 22209
©(703) 528-1818
Seeks to conserve America's natural resources through public education, citizen involvement, lobbying, and court action.

The Jane Goodall Institute for Wildlife Research, Education, and Conservation
P.O. Box 41720
Tucson, AZ 85717
©(602) 325-1211
Conducts research and works to protect wild and captive chimpanzees.

Land Trust Alliance
900 17th St., NW, Ste. 410
Washington, DC 20006-2596
©(202) 785-1410
An organization of local and regional conservation groups. Works to promote land conservation and expand land trusts.

League of Conservation Voters
1707 L St., NW, Ste. 550
Washington, DC 20036
©(202) 785-8683
Works to elect proenvironmental candidates to federal office.

LightHawk
P.O. Box 8163
Santa Fe, NM 87504
©(505) 982-9656
Provides conservation organizations with airborne transportation and other flight assistance.

Manomet Bird Observatory
P.O. Box 1770
Manomet, MA 02345
©(508) 224-6521
Engages in long-term research on wildlife populations as well as natural systems. Also sponsors a variety of educational programs, including training in field biology for college students.

Mission: Wolf
P.O. Box 211
Silver Cliff, CO 81249
©(719) 746-2919
Organization dedicated to the restoration of the wolf. Maintains a wolf sanctuary and promotes public education with a traveling wolf program.

Mississippi River Revival
P.O. Box 14702
Minneapolis, MN 55414
©(612) 339-4142
Works to protect and restore the Mississippi River through grassroots efforts.

National Arbor Day Foundation
211 N. 12th St., Ste. 501
Lincoln, NE 68508
©(402) 474-5655
An educational organization that sponsors tree planting in addition to a variety of other conservation projects.

National Audubon Society
950 Third Ave.
New York, NY 10022
©(212) 546-9100
Works for the conservation of wildlife and their habitats and also addresses other environmental issues through research, public education, lobbying, litigation, and citizen action.

National Coalition Against the Misuse of Pesticides
530 7th St., SE
Washington, DC 20001
©(202) 543-5450
Works for pesticide safety and the adoption of safer alternatives to pesticides. Supports research, promotes public awareness, and assists local action groups.

National Geographic Society
1145 17th St., NW
Washington, DC 20036
©(202) 857-7000
A scientific educational organization supporting environmental research.

National Institute for Urban Wildlife
10921 Trotting Ridge Way
Columbia, MD 21044
©(301) 596-3311
Conducts research and promotes methods of maintaining, enhancing, and controlling urban wildlife.

National Parks and Conservation Association
1015 31st St., NW
Washington, DC 20007
©(202) 944-8530
Dedicated to the protection and preservation of the U.S. National Park System.

National Wildflower Research Center
2600 FM 973 N
Austin, TX 78725-4201
©(512) 929-3600
Promotes the propagation and conservation of wildflowers and other native plants. Sponsors research and public outreach programs.

National Wildlife Federation
1400 16th St., NW
Washington, DC 20036
©(202) 797-6800
One of the largest environmental organizations in the United States. Promotes the wise use of natural resources through public education as well as through research programs and publications.

Natural Resources Defense Council
40 West 20th St.
New York, NY 10011
©(212) 727-2700
Works to protect the environment and public health through litigation, lobbying, and research.

The Nature Conservancy
1815 North Lynn St.
Arlington, VA 22209
©(703) 841-4860
An organization that attempts to preserve biological diversity by protecting land through purchase, gift, or cooperative management agreements. Manages over 1,000 nature sanctuaries.

The Nature Conservancy of Canada
794A Broadview Ave.
Ontario, Canada M4K 2P7
©(416) 469-1701
An organization that works with government, conservation groups, and individuals to acquire and preserve ecologically significant land in Canada.

North American Association for Environmental Education
P.O. Box 400
Troy, OH 45373
©(513) 698-6493
Promotes environmental education programs and serves as a network and information source for professionals in the field.

North American Native Fishes Association
123 W. Mt. Airy Ave.
Philadelphia, PA 19119
©(215) 247-0384
Promotes the conservation of and appreciation for native fish through observation and research; also disseminates information.

North American Wolf Society
P.O. Box 82950
Fairbanks, AK 99708
©(907) 474-6117
A group consisting of professional zoologists, lay conservationists, government agencies, and organizations working for the conservation of wolves and other wild canids.

Ocean Alliance
Building E, Fort Mason Center
San Francisco, CA 94123
©(415) 441-5970
An organization that is dedicated to protecting water resources and ocean life from pollution as well as other types of threats. Helps support public education and conservation programs.

Pacific Whale Foundation
Kealia Beach Plaza, Ste. 25
101 North Kihei Road
Kihei, Maui, HI 96753
©(808) 879-8811
©(800) 942-5311
Dedicated to saving endangered whales, dolphins, porpoises, and other marine mammals through research, conservation, and education programs.

The Peregrine Fund
5666 W. Flying Hawk Lane
Boise, ID 83709
©(208) 362-3716
Works to prevent the extinction of falcons and other birds of prey through research, captive breeding programs, and the reestablishment of native species.

Programme for Belize
P.O. Box 1088
Vineyard Haven, MA 02568
©(508) 693-0856
An organization that purchases tropical forest in Central America. Conducts research and works with the government of Belize to preserve land and train local citizens in conservation methods.

Rails-to-Trails Conservancy
1400 16th St., NW, Ste. 300
Washington, DC 20036
©(202) 797-5400
Converts abandoned railroad tracks to public trails for such uses as hiking, biking, cross-country skiing, and wildlife habitat.

Rainforest Action Network
450 Sansome, Ste. 700
San Francisco, CA 94111
©(415) 398-4404
An activist group that is dedicated to protecting rainforests around the world. Focuses on such issues as logging, ranching, international development bank activities, and rights of indigenous peoples.

Rainforest Alliance
270 Lafayette St., Ste. 512
New York, NY 10012
©(212) 941-1900
Seeks to raise awareness of the role the U.S. plays in tropical deforestation. Also works to promote the sustainable use of rainforests.

RARE Center for Tropical Bird Conservation
1529 Walnut St., 3rd Fl.
Philadelphia, PA 19102
©(215) 568-0420
Develops and funds projects to preserve endangered tropical bird species and their habitats in the Caribbean and Latin America.

Renew America
1400 16th St., NW, #710
Washington, DC 20036
©(202) 232-2252
Clearinghouse for environmental information that works for a sustainable society, giving information and recommendations to policy makers, environmental groups, and the media.

Rhino Rescue USA, Inc.
1150 17th St., NW, Ste. 400
Washington, DC 20036
©(202) 293-5305
Seeks to save rhinos from extinction. Funds rhino research and sanctuaries and fights illegal trade in rhino horn.

Rocky Mountain Elk Foundation
P.O. Box 8249
Missoula, MT 59807
©(406) 721-0010
Supports projects to conserve elk, other wildlife, and their habitats.

Rodale Institute
222 Main St.
Emmaus, PA 18098
©(215) 967-5171
Conducts research to develop environmentally sound farming and gardening methods. Sponsors educational programs and disseminates information.

The Ruffed Grouse Society
451 McCormick Road
Coraopolis, PA 15108
©(412) 262-4044
Works for the protection of ruffed grouse, American woodcock, and other forest wildlife and their habitat.

Save the Manatee Club
500 N. Maitland Ave.
Maitland, FL 32751
©(407) 539-0990
©(800) 432-JOIN
Seeks to protect the West Indian manatee, an endangered Florida marine mammal, through lobbying, research funding, and education.

Save-the-Redwoods League
114 Sansome St., Room 605
San Francisco, CA 94104
©(415) 362-2352
Purchases redwood groves and other trees for protection in parks, primarily in California. Supports reforestation, research, and education programs.

Save the Whales, Inc.
P.O. Box 2397
Venice, CA 90291
©(213) 392-6226
Works to preserve great whales and other marine mammals by educating the public and opposing commercial whaling and other threats.

Sea Shepherd Conservation Society
P.O. Box 7000-S
Redondo Beach, CA 90277
©(213) 373-6979
An activist organization that seeks to protect marine mammals through enforcement campaigns against illegal whaling and sealing.

Sierra Club
730 Polk St.
San Francisco, CA 94109
©(415) 776-2211
Dedicated to preserving wilderness areas and protecting the natural environment. Seeks to influence public policy decisions through legislative activities. Sponsors wilderness trips and other activities.

Sierra Club Legal Defense Fund
180 Montgomery St., 14th Fl.
San Francisco, CA 94104
©(415) 627-6700
Provides legal services to environmental groups in cases involving land use, public lands, pollution, endangered species, and wildlife habitats.

Smithsonian Institute
1000 Jefferson Drive, SW
Washington, DC 20560
©(202) 357-2700
Conducts scientific research, sponsors conservation programs, and develops national collections in natural history and anthropology.

Soil and Water Conservation Society
7515 NE Ankeny Road
Ankeny, IA 50021-9764
©(515) 289-2331
Promotes the conservation of soil, water, and related natural resources.

Student Conservation Association
P.O. Box 550
Charlestown, NH 03603
℅(603) 826-7755
Provides high school and college students with volunteer jobs in ecological restoration and related projects in national parks, wildlife refuges, and other conservation areas.

TreePeople
12601 Mulholland Drive
Beverly Hills, CA 90210
℅(818) 769-2663
Promotes tree planting and care in the Los Angeles area and sponsors tree propagation projects around the world.

Trout Unlimited
501 Church St., NE, Ste. 103
Vienna, VA 22180
℅(703) 281-1100
Seeks to preserve and improve trout, salmon, and steelhead habitat.

Union of Concerned Scientists
26 Church St.
Cambridge, MA 02238
℅(617) 547-5552
An organization of scientists and citizens concerned with the impact of advanced technology on society. Focuses on national energy policy, national security policy, and nuclear power safety.

U.S. Public Interest Research Group (PIRG)
215 Pennsylvania Ave., SE
Washington, DC 20003
℅(202) 546-9707
Conducts research and engages in lobbying for consumer and environmental protection.

University Research Expeditions Program
Desk H11
University of California
Berkeley, CA 94720
℅(510) 642-6586
Recruits volunteers for field research projects in environmental, natural, and social sciences.

Whitetails Unlimited
P.O. Box 422
Sturgeon Bay, WI 54235
℅(414) 743-6777
Promotes sound deer management; sponsors research and public awareness programs.

Wilderness Society
900 17th St., NW
Washington, DC 20006
℅(202) 833-2300
An organization that is dedicated to the protection of wildlands and wildlife. Focuses primarily on public lands, including national forests and parks, wildlife refuges, and Bureau of Land Management lands.

Wildlife Conservation International
c/o New York Zoological Society
Bronx, NY 10460
℅(212) 220-5155
Dedicated to saving critical habitats, ecosystems, and species around the world. Supports field research and training and advises on protected area management.

Wildlife Information Center
629 Green St.
Allentown, PA 18102
℅(215) 434-1637
A wildlife protection organization that focuses primarily on birds of prey. Disseminates information about wildlife conservation and also conducts a variety of educational programs.

The Wildlife Society
5410 Grosvenor Lane
Bethesda, MD 20814
℅(301) 897-9770
A professional organization of biologists, resource managers, and other individuals that are interested in resource conservation and wildlife management. Provides information on issues pertaining to wildlife conservation.

The Wolf Fund
P.O. Box 471
Moose, WY 83012
℅(307) 733-0740
An organization that is dedicated to the reintroduction of the gray wolf into the Greater Yellowstone Ecosystem.

World Aquaculture Society
Louisiana State University
16 E. Fraternity
Baton Rouge, LA 70803
℅(504) 388-3137
Promotes, evaluates, and disseminates information pertaining to the development of aquaculture around the world.

World Forestry Center
4033 SW Canyon Road
Portland, OR 97221
℅(503) 228-1367
Promotes forest preservation, serving as an information clearinghouse.

World Resources Institute
1709 New York Ave., NW, Ste. 700
Washington, DC 20006
℅(202) 638-6300
A research and policy institute that addresses the need for the sustainable use of natural resources.

World Society for the Protection of Animals
29 Perkins St.
P.O. Box 190
Boston, MA 02130
℅(617) 522-7000
Works to aid animals, especially during and after natural disasters.

Worldwatch Institute
1776 Massachusetts Ave., NW
Washington, DC 20036
℅(202) 452-1999
Informs policymakers and the public about environmental issues and their relationship to the global economy.

World Wide Fund for Nature
Avenue du Mont-Blanc
1196 Gland
Geneva
Switzerland
022 64 9111
Promotes conservation of wildlife and wild lands and the wise use of the earth's resources.

World Wildlife Fund
1250 24th St., NW
Washington, DC 20037
℅(202) 293-4800
Works to preserve endangered wildlife and wild lands through sustainable development and biodiversity.

Xerces Society
10 SW Ash St.
Portland, OR 97204
℅(503) 222-2788
Seeks to prevent the extinction of rare invertebrates and their habitats.

Zero Population Growth
1400 16th St., NW, Ste. 320
Washington, DC 20036
℅(202) 332-2200
Raises awareness of the need for a sustainable balance between population, environment, and resources.

CHILDREN'S ORGANIZATIONS

Elsa Clubs of America (ELSA)
P.O. Box 4572
North Hollywood, CA 91617-0572
℅(818) 761-8387
An organization sponsored by Elsa Wild Animal Appeal. Dedicated to educating young people about the environment, with an emphasis on wildlife.

Kids for a Clean Environment
P.O. Box 158254
Nashville, TN 37215
℅(615) 331-0708
Provides children with environmental information and projects.

Kids for Conservation—Today and Tomorrow
Illinois Department of Conservation
524 S. 2nd St.
Springfield, IL 62701
℅(217) 524-4126
A family-oriented environmental club for children ages 3 to 15.

Kids S.T.O.P.
P.O. Box 471
Forest Hills, NY 11375
℅(718) 997-7387
An ecology club for elementary-age children.

Ranger Rick's Nature Club
8925 Leesburg Pike
Vienna, VA 22184
℅(703) 790-4000
The children's division of the National Wildlife Federation. Dedicated to teaching children to respect living things and to conserve natural resources.

GOVERNMENT & INDEPENDENT ORGANIZATIONS

UNITED STATES

Bureau of Land Management
Department of the Interior
18th and C Sts., NW, Room 5600
Washington, DC 20240
©(202) 208-5717
Administers the 272 million-plus acres of U.S. public lands under multiple-use principles, including outdoor recreation, fish and wildlife protection, livestock grazing, timber, and industrial development.

Department of Energy
Forrestal Building
1000 Independence Ave., SW
Washington, DC 20585
©(202) 586-8800
Coordinates and administers the energy functions of the federal government. Responsibilities include long-term, high-risk research and development of energy technology, energy conservation, and nuclear weapons program.

Environmental Protection Agency
401 M St., SW
Washington, DC 20460
©(202) 260-2090
Independent agency that establishes and enforces U.S. environmental standards. Conducts research on environmental problems, including air and water pollution and management and cleanup of solid and hazardous wastes. Assists state and local governments.

Forest Service
Department of Agriculture
Auditors Bldg., 201, 4th Fl., NW
14th St., NW
Washington, DC 20250
©(202) 205-1760
Administers national forests and grasslands and manages resources in them. Also conducts research in forestry and wildlife management.

National Marine Fisheries Service
Department of Commerce
Metro One Bldg., Room 9334
1320 East-West Hwy.
Silver Spring, MD 20910
©(301) 713-2239
Conducts research and works to conserve ocean resources within 200 miles of U.S. coasts.

National Oceanic and Atmospheric Administration
Department of Commerce
Rockville, MD 20852
©(301) 443-8910
Works to improve the environment and oceanic life, providing information on the effects of human actions on the environment.

National Park Service
Department of the Interior
1849 C St., NW, Room 3104
Washington, DC 20240
©(202) 208-6843
Administers parks and monuments and manages landmarks programs for natural and historic properties.

National Science Foundation
Washington, DC 20550
©(202) 357-9498
Initiates and supports scientific research and develops science education programs.

Soil Conservation Service
Department of Agriculture
14th St. and Independence Ave., SW
Washington, DC 20250
©(202) 447-4543
Provides technical and educational assistance with projects involving watersheds, flood protection, water supply and management, recreation, and wildlife habitats.

U.S. Fish and Wildlife Service
Department of the Interior
1849 C St., NW, Room 3012
Washington, DC 20240
©(202) 208-4717
Office of Endangered Species:
©(703) 358-2171
Works to conserve and protect fish and wildlife and their habitats. Enforces the Endangered Species Act, Lacey Act, Marine Mammal Protection Act, and Migratory Bird Treaty Act.

U.S. Geological Survey
National Center
12201 Sunrise Valley Drive
Reston, VA 22092
©(703) 648-4000
Conducts research in geology, hydrology, geography, and related sciences. Publishes maps and reports on the nation's mineral, fuel, and water resources and physical features.

CANADA

Department of Conservation and Protection
Place Vincent Massey
Hull, Quebec, Canada K1A 1G5
Mailing address:
Ottawa, Ontario, Canada K1A OH3
Responsible for operational and research activities pertaining to Inland Waters Directorate, Canadian Wildlife Service, and Environmental Protection Directorate.

Department of Fisheries and Oceans
200 Kent St.
Ottawa, Ontario
Canada K1A OE6
Responsibilities include fisheries development and management, fisheries research, oceanography, hydrography, and administration of small craft harbors.

Forestry Canada/Forêts Canada
Place Vincent Massey
351 St. Joseph Blvd.
Hull, Quebec, Canada K1A 1G5
©(819) 997-1107
Coordinates forestry policy and related matters in Canada. Conducts research and provides information and technical services to governments, industry, and the public.

INTERNATIONAL

Commission on National Parks and Protected Areas
IUCN Headquarters
CH-1196 Gland
Switzerland
©022-64-91-14
Division of World Conservation Union that carries out activities concerning national parks as well as other protected lands.

Convention on International Trade in Endangered Species of Wild Fauna and Flora
6, rue du Maupas
Case Postale 78
CH-1000 9 Lausanne
Switzerland
©21-200081
An organization of over 90 member countries that monitors and regulates trade of wild plants and animals.

Inter-American Tropical Tuna Commission
c/o Scripps Institution of Oceanography
La Jolla, CA 92093
©(619) 546-7100
Works to conserve the tuna and dolphin resources in the eastern Pacific. Member nations include the United States, Costa Rica, France, Japan, Nicaragua, and Panama.

International Whaling Commission
135 Station Road
Histon
Cambridge CB4 4NP
England, U.K.
©0223-233971
Intergovernmental organization that monitors the whaling industry, reviews whale protection measures, and disseminates information on whales.

United Nations Environment Programme
Regional office for North America:
2 United Nations Plaza, Rm. DC2-303
New York, NY 10017
©(212) 963-8093
Promotes protection of natural resources and environmentally sound development. Works with UN agencies, governments, and organizations on problems such as ozone depletion, acid rain, and desertification.

World Conservation Monitoring Centre
219 Huntington Road
Cambridge CB3 0DL
England, U.K.
©0223-277314
Provides a conservation information service, integrating monitoring activities on animal and plant species, critical conservation sites, protected areas, and wildlife trade.

World Conservation Union
(formerly International Union for the Conservation of Nature and Natural Resources)
Avenue du Mont-Blanc
CH-1196 Gland
Switzerland
©022-64-91-14
Alliance of organizations in over 120 countries working for natural resource conservation. Maintains a global network of scientists and professionals.

ACKNOWLEDGMENTS

Jill Bailey has written more than 40 children's books and several adult books. She has also written and produced videos for the BBC, some of which have won awards.

John Birdsall is a freelance writer and editor specializing in wildlife and conservation topics.

Hanna Bolus is a freelance writer and editor on international environmental issues.

Duncan Brewer is a full-time writer. His specializations include natural history, earth sciences, Third World issues, and investigative journalism.

Michael Bright is a managing editor with the BBC's world-renowned Natural History Unit in Bristol. He is the producer of numerous wildlife and conservation books, including *The Private Life of Birds* (1993).

Helen Clapperton is a trainee solicitor at Frere Cholmeley Solicitors, London. She has spent the last few months with the Foundation for International Environmental Law and Development, based at the School of Law, Kings College London, London University.

Mark Cocker is a professional author and naturalist.

Catherine Dold is a contributing writer for *The New York Times* specializing in environmental subjects. She has been an editor of *Audubon* magazine and a staff writer for the Natural Resources Defense Council.

Jonathan Elphick is a natural history editor, consultant, and author who has written regularly on birds for the *Wildlife Fact File.*

John Farrand, Jr., has developed three bird guides and written six other books on natural history subjects, as well as numerous magazine articles. He currently serves as an editorial adviser and regular contributor to *American Birds,* a magazine of the National Audubon Society.

Sarah Foster is a journalist with a special interest in the environment. She is also an experienced scuba diver and recently spent five months in Central America, where she was involved in marine conservation work.

Jeff Hall is a writer, photographer, professional tour guide, and whale researcher, working in Alaska, California, and Baja California, as well as the deserts and mountains of the southwestern United States.

John Hechtel is a specialist in bear behavior, ecology, and conservation who has worked for the Alaska Department of Fish and Game since 1980. He has been involved in research on bears for over 17 years, including grizzly, black, and polar bears. He is also a writer and photographer, and he has served as an adviser to television productions created by National Geographic as well as the BBC.

Sue Heinemann is a writer, editor, and photographer who has recently worked on the *Wildlife Fact File.*

Suzanne Jones is a writer and editor who has recently been involved with the *Wildlife Fact File.*

Dr. R. E. Kenward was born into a farming family in 1949, then took Honors and Doctoral degrees at Oxford University, and currently studies birds of prey for the Institute of Terrestrial Ecology. With over 50 scientific publications, including books on goshawks and radio-tagging, he is a director-at-large of the Raptor Research Foundation and a Fellow of the Linnean Society.

Fred Pearce is an environmental journalist and author specializing in international issues. He is the author of books on the greenhouse effect and acid rain, as well as environmental campaigns.

Alice Quine is a writer and editor who specializes in educational materials and has recently worked on the *Wildlife Fact File.*

Nigel Sitwell edited *Wildlife* magazine (now renamed *BBC Wildlife*) for 16 years and currently travels around the world reporting on wildlife and the environment.

Craig Tufts directs the National Wildlife Federation's Backyard Wildlife Habitat Program and serves as its chief naturalist. He and his family share their yard with hummingbirds, hawks, butterflies, turtles, and over 100 native plant species.

David Unwin studied pterosaurs for his Ph.D. at Reading University and is currently a Royal Society Research Fellow at Bristol University. At present he is working on fossil birds, baby ichthyosaurs, and the wings of pterosaurs—the latter in conjunction with a Russian paleontologist, N. N. Bakhurina, to whom he is married. During the next year he intends to search for dinosaurs and pterosaurs in western Mongolia.

Jeremy West is a professional sound recordist who specializes in wildlife and natural history recordings as well as preparing live soundtrack for adventure documentary films.

PICTURE CREDITS

Abbreviations:
t—top; b—bottom; l—left; r—right

Animals Animals/Earth Scenes M. Dick 28

Ardea London Ltd. 114b; B. Y. Arthus 190b; I. Beames 103tl; R. Bunge 66br; J. Daniels 52b; J. P. Ferrero 19br, 97; B. Gibbons 117bl; F. Gohier 32b, 35t, 106tl, 123b; C. Haagner 99br; P. Morris 171t; E. Parer-Cook 11tl, 119, 158–159, 171b; J. Player 50

David Robert Austen 93, 96bl, 98

R. Barnwell 186tl, 189t

Bavarian State Collection 54t

Bruce Coleman Ltd. 29t; J. & D. Bartlett 166tr; A. Compost 26b; M. Fogden 67tl, 124b; J. Foott 2–3, 19tl, 35b; M. Freeman 52tl, 82b; C. B. Frith 24, 25; Frithfoto 27t; F. Futil 143b; S. Krasemann 16tl; F. Lanting 117tr; L. C. Marigo 126tl; J. Murray 73br; D. & M. Plage 110; H. Reinhard 11tr; K. Taylor 45, 47t, 192; R. Williams 76b, 125, 128b, 144, 145b, 189br; G. Zeisler 38, 42t, 44t

Martyn Cowley 56b

Daniel J. Cox 12tl, 13, 14bl, 15tr, 18bl, 161tl

Earthwatch Europe M. Christie 69tr; A. Schreeber 109t; Smith 123tl

Victor Englebert 94t, 95b

Mary Evans Picture Library 178bl, 179tr

P. S. Fieldhouse 90tr

Frank Lane Picture Agency D. Grewcock 113br; P. Heard 37; E. & D. Hosking 51tr, 108tl, 161b, 191br; F. Polking 115; Silvestris 21, 67br; W. Wisniewski 186b

Greenpeace 155tr; Dom 157b4; Dorreboon 153; Franks 157b1; Leitinger 155b; Morgan 152tl, 152bl, 156b; Morris 154; Olsen 157b2; Pahlich 157b3; Van de Bunt 156tl

John Hechtel 16br

The Image Bank Artphotopolke 75; De Moura Machado 112; S. Wilkinson 157tl

JWPT J. Hartley 170, 173br; P. Trenchard 161tr, 168tl; W. R. Wood 169

The Mansell Collection 179tl

Mark Twain Memorial, Hartford, CT 139br

David M. Martill 58t, 59br

National Wildlife Federation 7, 147

The Natural History Museum, London 174tl, 174bl, 175, 176tl, 176br, 177tr, 177br, 178tr, 178tl, 179b

Natural Science Photos J. C. Pasieka 145t

Nature Photographers Ltd. R. Tidman 85tr

NHPA ANT 22; H. Ausloos 142; A. Bannister 163, 164br, 166bl; B. Beehler 29b; G. I. Bernard 23b; N. Callow 104bl; G. Cambridge 20tl; L. Campbell 167br; D. Currey 142tr; S. Dalton 20b, 40tl, 41, 46, 64, 105tl, 111b; B. Hawkes 188; H. Ingen 96tr; S. Krasemann 14t; T. McDonald 82t; H. Palo 114tl, 120–121; J. Sauvanet 23t; J. Shaw 17t; K. Switak 116

Oxford Scientific Films A. Bannister 92bl; D. Fox 51b; H. Hall 118; A. MacEwen 6; OSF/Okapia A. Shah 107; S. Osolinski 123tr; S. Pilkington 70–71; A. Shay 53b; K. Westerskov 85b, 86bl, 87br

Photo Researchers A. Carey 63tl, 132bl; B. Curtsinger 146; D. Faulkner 180tl, 181, 182t, 182b, 184, 185tl, 185b; J. Ferrara 134tl; K. Fink 134bl; L. Georgia 149; F. Gohier 151; J. Halaska 139tl; G. Haling 90b; Kirtley-Perkins 148tl; P. & T Leeson 88tl, 89; B. Lehnhausen 148b; J. Lepore 61, 130tl, 132tl; A. Martinez 183t; Maslowski 131; T. McHugh 62, 63br; A. Mercieca 105br; J. Mitchell 135; R. Planck 102; J. H. Robinson 150; L. L. Rue 60, 100tl; J. Serrao 101; R. Smith 133; Southern Living 136bl; D. Suzio 88bl; Van Bucher 138

Planet Earth Pictures S. Avery 172; D. Barrett 84; M. Clay 66tl; R. Coomber 36b; G. Douwma 43b; J. Downer 39t; C. Farnetti 44b; P. Folkens 30; H. Heap 49; J. Lythgoe 73bl, 95tr; D. Maitland 81tl, 138; M. Mattock 36tl; D. Perrine 11b; D. A. Ponton 113tl; K. Puttock 4; D. E. Romley 129br; K. Scholey 86t, 103br; J. Scott 47b, 190t, 108br, 111t, 165tr, 187; N. Sefton 140bl; H. Voigtmann 80

Rex Features Ltd. Keystone 79t

Kevin Schafer & Martha Hill Photographers © K. Schafer 8, 79b, 124tl, 127tr, 127bl, 128tr, 129l

P. Schollmeier 137

Science Photo Library M. Dohrn/S. Winkworth 57t

Spooner/Gamma R. Gaillard R. 65, 68, 69bl; A. Ribeiro 74tl

Still Pictures D. Dancer 78; M. Edwards 73t, 76, 77, 81b

Streano/Havens © V. Streano 31, 33t, 33b, 34b

Survival Anglia Ltd. R. Price 141

Tom Stack & Associates M. Nilsen 83; T. Tackett 99tl

U.S. Army Corps of Engineers 183b

VIREO A. Morris 39b; J. West 162tl, 164tl

Zefa Picture Library T. van Sant/Geosphere Project Endpapers

INDEX